Schools Flunk—

Kids Don't

Schools Flunk—

Kids Don't

A practical guide for parents,
teachers, principals, community
leaders, and students who want
to turn their school around.

Dr. Joe Petterle

Griffin Publishing
Glendale, California

10   9   8   7   6   5   4   3   2   1

ISBN 1-882180-16-X

Cover Design: Sarah Petterle

Griffin Publishing
544 Colorado Street
Glendale, California 91204

Manufactured in the United States of America.

CONTENTS

This book is dedicated
with heartfelt thanks to:

John, Dudley, Ben, Larry, Jack, Sylvia, Matt, Clarence, Bill, Chuck, Tom, Tim, Lloyd, Francis, Sarge, Pete, John, Mike, George, Dave, Agnes Claire, Laetitia, Kelley, George, Ray, Jim, Larry, Mike, Stan, Chet, Pete, Lois, Vince, Roger, Don, Chan, Eleanor, Pete, Ron, Jack, Bob, Jean, Audrey, Phyllis, Earl, Pam, Alan, Marshall, Nancy, Bart, Marty, Joe, John, Sarah, Kate, Champ, Barbara, Dick, Lane, Angel, Dick, Pamela, Dorothy, Pat, Vic, Joanne, Edie, Paul, Brenda, Jack, Jim, Fred, Vern, Bob, Bart, Jim, Jon, Kent, Dan, Fannie, Elmo, Kay, Bob, Mae, Steve, Carol, Bev, Sarah, Nancy, Annalee, Penne, Sue, Jackie, John, Keith, and Annie—My Teachers

My thanks to the staffs at Yuba City, Tamalpais, El Molino, and El Camino, and all of the wonderful teachers, administrations, parents, and students I've met throughout this exciting journey.

A very special thanks to Mae Jarman; without her energy, assistance, optimism, and tireless effort, this book would still be stacked in a series of jumbled piles behind my desk.

From the *Los Angeles Times*, January 20, 1993—

At least 800 gang-related killings occurred in Los Angeles
County in 1992, law enforcement officials said.

These are our children and this is *their* time...
the crime, the drugs, the violence;
the helpless, the hopeless, the homeless...
the despair and cynicism that have replaced
the American dream...
institutions, ideas, and traditions that no longer
inspire; that no longer work.

But we still have the power, working locally, to
turn things around, to take back our
neighborhoods.

Like the original American Revolution,
this too must be a grassroots enterprise;
and the logical place to start is with the
schools...

What more noble endeavor than to seek to turn
our children's world around?

Joe Petterle,
1993

PREFACE

By 1972, Joe Petterle had worked his way through the educational structure—teacher, coach, dean, assistant principal—and had become the youngest high school principal in the State of California. Later, as a central office administrator, however, he became disillusioned in his attempts to turn schools around. So in the spring of 1979, he personally took over the reins of a troubled high school to pilot a school-change process which combined organizational behavior concepts, change theory, human interaction principles, and failure-avoidance technology.

As he later wrote:

> I embarked upon the journey of a lifetime. What seemed to be at first glance an impossible situation turned out to be what any educator dreams of—
>
> "Turn this high school around—or close it," the school board said. "You have one year."
>
> Over the course of that year and throughout subsequent years, I watched those so-called "burned-out" teachers and those "turned-off" staff come together and create a school that worked. I saw a complacent community coalesce behind the school and embrace it with an intensely personal dedication, And I saw disconnected, apathetic kids, suddenly grab hold of this new lifeline called school.
>
> But most important, I saw **change**. Bold, daring, earthshaking, risk-filled change. Not just change that looks good or feels good; but hard change, tough change, gut-wrenching change; focused with the intensity of a laser beam on a common purpose and a common goal. Change organized around a central theme of "what's good for kids." Change driven by a sense of urgency and commitment—"whatever it takes."

A year later, the school's turnaround was being cited as a "real life" example of educational reform. The *Washington Post* cited the innovative discipline policy as the reason for success. The *Associated Press* looked at the amazing academic turnaround. Local press and T.V. coverage marveled at the positive teacher attitude and subsequent rush to enroll in "a school that works."

On December 8, 1983, President Ronald Reagan, in his address to the National Forum on Excellence in Education, stated:

In my home state of California, El Camino High, in Sacramento, used to suffer from all the ills that plague so many schools—drugs and alcohol abuse, poor attendance, declining enrollment, low achievement. And then, El Camino Principal, Joe Petterle, and the Board of Education put together a program designed to stress the fundamentals. Today, achievement at El Camino is climbing. The daily student absence rate has dropped from 14 percent to under 4 percent, and the school has its maximum enrollment of 1,700 students and a waiting list of almost 400.

Working with over 175 schools nationwide since 1986 in a variety of settings as President of SAGE EDUCATION, Dr. Petterle can attest to the effectiveness of this school-change model. "I've witnessed varying degrees of success and failure. I've seen real transformations and 'going through the motions.' Through these experiences, I have come a great distance in understanding what it takes for schools to change," he notes. "But I have not wavered from my original belief, validated by experience, that **schools can change!**"

"Beginning with basic premises—affirmed in research and experience," Dr. Petterle argues, "...

1. All children can learn
2. Teachers can teach
3. The school is the variable

...I have come to truly believe that **Schools Flunk...Kids Don't**, and that you can change this variable—the school—if you want to badly enough."

Dr. Petterle, however, insists that:

> Only those with a personal stake in the school—parents, teachers, administrators, students—can change it.

In these pages you will find practical, down-to-earth examples of what can happen in schools when those most affected take charge. You will also find a step-by-step process to take your school from where it is now to where you want it to be.

"The school," Dr. Petterle asserts, "can be the focal point for the resurgence and revitalization of the American community. It is the place to start."

Richard Dean Burns, PhD
Claremont, California

"Still crazy after all these years."
Paul Simon

INTRODUCTION

This book is not about education; it is about schools. And not just any "school," your school. I am here to tell you to forget about changing education or "schools across the country," because it can't be done—at least not as it's depicted. But you can change your school. In fact, you can make it better than you or anyone around you ever imagined.

I am convinced, after being in hundreds of schools across the country, that the only way to change schools is one at a time. And the only people who can change schools are those with the most at stake...people like you: the parents, teachers, principals, community leaders, and yes, the students.

Described in these pages are some of the real-life kinds of things that have happened in schools. Giant positive strides in changing how a school does business. And I'll tell you how you can replicate these things in your school.

The examples are from real life. They happened. Some will question the underlying theoretical foundations; others the research base. All I know is that I've been there and they happened.

But I'll also warn you again. Changing schools is for zealots, for mavericks. You've got to want it badly, you've got to be willing to put it on the line. Remember, if changing your school were easy, somebody already would have done it.

So you see, I'm here to foment a revolution. A school revolution—a grassroots uprising—fueled by ideas that work and initiated by people like you who want the best for the kids of America.

For while changing schools is not easy, it is possible, more possible than you ever thought. And...just think of it...when you change a school, you change not only an institution, you change the lives of thousands of young people who will move through that school year after year. You become the "Modern American Hero."

Come take a look then, at what I call nitty-gritty, nuts-and-bolts school reform. You won't find any legislative proposals; no governor's blue ribbon committees. But you will find plenty of stuff you can get your hands on—stuff you can really make happen in your school. Stuff that makes the difference.

I

LET'S BEGIN

- *OBSERVATION: If All Children Can Learn...*
  Why Can't All Children Learn Algebra?

- *SCHOOLS NEED A CHANGE PROCESS*

> ...We have [now] come to understand that under appropriate
> learning conditions, students differ in the rate at which they can
> learn—not in the level to which they can achieve or in their basic
> capacity to learn...
>
> > Benjamin Bloom
> > *All Our Children Learning* 1981

OBSERVATION:

If All Children Can Learn...
Why Can't All Children Learn Algebra?

Imagine this. You've just left the doctor's office. After a
thorough examination of your child—blood tests, x-rays, the
works—the doctor has informed you that your child has a rare
disease. Your child, he tells you, will die in four years; or, at
best, survive in illness and pain for the rest of his life. There is
no cure, your doctor says, unless...

You cling to this word, "unless." Unless what? Unless
anything! I will do anything you say, anything! The doctor tells
you that the next nine months are critical. This is your one and
only chance. He explains that you must drastically change your
child's diet, subject him to radiation, and provide six hours per
day of intense physical therapy.

Are you willing to make this kind of an effort, you are
asked? Are you kidding—when do we start!

Nine months of intense effort in exchange for a normal
life—a bargain. Yet schools, in a slightly different context, pass
up this "life-saving" bargain. The constraints of the structure of
the typical high school, for example, simply do not allow it to
make "an intense nine-month effort," regardless of the resulting
consequences.

Let me explain.

A number of years ago, we began looking at the
transcripts—the academic records—of the young people who
were going through our high school. We found a significant

correlation between the degree of success in algebra and the degree of success in the student's high school career. Taking this a step further, what we were really finding—scary as it might seem—was a correlation between what the student achieved in algebra and what the student ultimately achieved in life!

In other words, we could predict, with a high degree of certainty, that a student who failed, or did not take algebra, would in fact do poorly throughout the remainder of his or her high school career. It follows, of course, as well-documented fact, that students who do poorly in high school, and/or do not complete high school, typically end up at the lower end of the socioeconomic scale. (For every one Horatio Alger story, there are millions of case studies to document the obvious fact that non-high school graduates simply do not do as well.)

Imagine then, our concern as we went through transcript after transcript looking at a child's academic record and moving very quickly to algebra. Once we knew the grade in algebra (or whether the student had even taken algebra), we could predict with confidence what the rest of the grades would be like, whether the student would transition to college, and the extent to which he or she would be successful in college.

Since our first experience with what we call the "algebra phenomenon," we have found, time and time again, that this basic rule holds true. Show me how a student fared in algebra and I'll tell you how the student fared in the remainder of his or her academic career. *Algebra*, in other words, is a "gatekeeper" course!

We immediately took this new insight to the math departments in the university system. They simply looked at us, smiled, and said, "Some kids have it and some kids don't." Or, to paraphrase, all children *can't* learn.

We went to the high school math teachers and got a similar response. "How can you expect these kids to learn when they don't have the basic skills to add, subtract, multiply, or divide, let alone think in quantitative terms and understand concepts like x^2?"

We returned to the facts. The transcripts. The academic records. Each time we looked at them, they frightened us more. Just like the doctor, we had our "test results." And the prognosis from these results was that many of our kids' futures were "terminal." No college; no economic success; no job security; no American Dream. And, as well-intentioned as our thinking was—as good as it sounded—"All children can learn"—the facts led to a different conclusion. We had two choices: either abandon our basic premise (and a large segment of the kids); or amend it. After some review, a check of the research, and much soul searching, we proceeded to issue a corollary to our basic premise. We said:

"All children can learn and that means that all children can learn algebra; what some children can't do is learn algebra as it is currently structured within the organizational design of the typical high school."

In other words, if we continue to assume that the school is a constant in its organizational structure, then indeed all children cannot, and, indeed, some children will not learn algebra. But if we believe that the school is a variable and can change and adapt its delivery system, then, indeed, all children can learn algebra.

The problem, of course, is that schools expect all children to learn algebra under the same conditions. It isn't just that we expect them to learn; we expect them to learn algebra as everyone else has learned it: in 180 school days; in 50-minute class periods; using the traditional textbook; each day meeting in a class of 30; with an overworked, and sometimes, uninspired instructor.

These are the express "conditions" we put on learning algebra. We expect students to compete with each other for grades, and to have their learning tied very closely to the condition of time. So we tell a student, "If you have not learned Chapter 4 by the end of this week, you will not learn Chapter 4 ever because the rest of the class is moving on." We say further,

> If you do not bring the necessary basic knowledge to the classroom, you cannot learn algebra. Do not expect us to spend extra time and energy helping you because your knowledge level deviates from the norm, and if you cannot move as fast as the others do, you must be left behind.

We should also say to these children that because we are not willing to redesign how we deliver education to them, or because we don't know any better way, we are condemning them to a life less fulfilling, less satisfying, less economically advantaged because, at age 14, they couldn't make it in algebra.

But again, what if we truly believe that the school is a variable—that it can change how it operates. And, what if, through our independent research, (subsequently documented at numerous high schools) algebra truly is a pivotal course. Can the school refocus and reshape itself when it knows—when it understands—how important algebra is to the future of its students?

What if we could change the system so that all children were successful in algebra? Couldn't we similarly predict, with a high degree of probability, their subsequent success in school and life? WOW!

The answer is yes, and here's how it works. When a school believes that algebra or, for that matter, any other course is pivotal to the well-being of each and every student, then that school can develop an organizational structure which will ensure that all children are successful. It can; the question is whether it will.

Take an incoming class of 9th graders and convince them and their parents that each and every one of them will successfully complete algebra.

"Every 9th grader who attends this school will successfully complete algebra."

That's the easy part. Now go to the staff. This represents a tremendous mindshift, a new paradigm for the staff. No longer can they say, "Some kids have it, some kids don't." Rather, they must say, "All kids have it, but the school doesn't...and since it is a matter of no small importance to our students, we will develop a system whereby all students will be successful in algebra." Now imagine how this would look in the real life day-to-day operations of a high school.

The fifteen percent of the 9th graders who normally take algebra and successfully master it would be unaffected. They would enroll in the regular algebra class, navigate effectively through the learning conditions, survive, and even prosper.

The five percent who normally fail algebra and the thirty percent who would take a watered-down pre-algebra are also enrolled in the regular algebra class. In addition, however, they would simultaneously be enrolled in "algebra assistance"—a course designed to take them through the same lesson, but with additional explanation, time for questions, and help from three volunteer assistants in the class. By the end of each daily session, most would understand what had been taught that day in the regular algebra class and would have completed and checked their homework assignments.

Another thirty percent of the 9th graders traditionally take "high school" or "bonehead" math. This is a basic arithmetic class for students who have not mastered the skills necessary to "move-on." Most of them never move on, but end up taking four years of "bonehead" math (if they stick around that long) and never really understand how to do long division.

These students are also enrolled in the regular class! In addition, they attend "algebra assistance" and another class called "algebra basic skills" where they quickly learn how to multiply 4x times 3x. Their growth in basic skills is dramatic because they are not being taught in a vacuum. Rather they are learning within the context of something that is important and meaningful to them—their success in algebra.

Finally, the lowest twenty percent who, in previous years, have been enrolled in special remediation math (where even lower level skills are taught but seemingly never mastered) are put into the same sequence of classes: algebra, algebra assistance, algebra basic skills...and yes, another class, algebra basic skills reinforcement, where they log an hour a day on a computer driving home basic skills.

Take a look at what we have: some students taking four periods of algebra, others three, others two! Imagine the drain on staff time and energy, the need for retraining, as we put aside for the time being, other courses like world history and English to focus on algebra. Imagine the resentment of some teachers who believed from the beginning that this experiment was impossible. The good news is that numerous schools (holding true to the premise that all children can learn, and that it is the school's task to vary the conditions to enable children to learn) have actually set about making all 9th graders successful in algebra, using variations on the approach described here.

The side benefits of such a change are in themselves amazing. A new level of self-esteem develops simply by having all students carry algebra books around. A new sense of teacher effectiveness emanates from the concept that it is not, *if* the student can learn, but *when* the student will learn. Heretofore unheard of progress in the attainment of basic skills is greeted with a sense of shock and amazement.

If and when the school decides to provide an intense dose of the medicine the children need, many current and future problems can be eliminated. The high school student who cannot read, for example, typically takes one class (50 minutes) of remedial reading each day. Then, this student proceeds to history class, English class, science class with little chance of ever deciphering those textbooks. Why not an intense dose of reading, 4, 5, or even 6 hours a day for two, or three months until the child masters reading?

That's all it would take. The child would have attained reading skills for life. But, to attempt this type of revolutionary plan requires a change in the structure of the school. How do we go about changing the structure of the school to fit the needs of students? Where do we start? Read on...!

The significant problems we face cannot be solved at the same level of thinking we were at when we created them.

Albert Einstein

SCHOOLS NEED A CHANGE PROCESS

The algebra example described actually depicted a method of "beating the system" while maintaining the structure. Note that the basic structure, the 6 or 7 period day, 50 minute classes, meeting five days a week was not disturbed. A few, more bold and courageous, have replaced or redesigned this structure to eliminate many of the insurmountable conditions typically placed on learning algebra.

But this brings us to the real heart of the issue. Most schools won't even attempt this type of radical change within the structure, let alone consider redesigning the structure itself. Where does one start? How do teachers and administrators go about it? Can the system really change?

"Doesn't this rank up there with doing battle with windmills? Who am I (are we) to think I can make an impact...and where will I ever find the time or the energy, let alone the knowledge to bring about this kind of change...."

The fact is, most teachers and administrators (contrary to much popular rhetoric) perform their tasks well under trying conditions. They know how to teach within the burdensome constraints of the typical classroom and they know how to run schools in the manner schools have always been run.

What they don't know how to do is *change* schools. While the education reform movement has focused tremendous pressure on teachers and administrators, the fact remains that they do not have the training or experience to understand the complexities of organizational change. The reality is that we are not talking simple, basic little changes; we're talking dismantle and restructure—we're talking major overhaul of a tradition-bound, 100-year-old way of doing things!

Quite simply, if we want to open the door for the algebra-type changes we've seen here, we need to give schools a change process.

II

PRECONDITIONS FOR SCHOOL CHANGE

In some instances, even a change process is not enough. We have found, through trial and error, that certain conditions must exist within a school if change is to have a chance. These "preconditions" are:

- ❏ Local Autonomy
- ❏ Leadership Growth Potential
- ❏ Staff Readiness

The key is to avoid embarking on the complex journey of change before checking the condition of the vehicle you'll be driving. You can't make it from New York to San Francisco in a '57 Edsel (at least, you can't count on making it). You'll run into real difficulty getting spare parts. The odds are, you'll have to jerryrig repairs. At the very least, you'll make the journey more difficult and keep the outcome in doubt. Driving across the country is hard enough without adding the pressure and worry of a car not designed for the rigors of the journey. And so it is with school change.

There are no absolute "scores" to achieve in each area. Rather, minimum levels must be attained in order to keep the odds on your side. The following describes the three preconditions, a method for assessing the existing level of each, and suggested developmental processes for improving the existing levels.

STAFF READINESS

LEADERSHIP GROWTH POTENTIAL

LOCAL AUTONOMY

THE FOUNDATION FOR SCHOOL CHANGE

Precondition A:
Local Autonomy

- *OBSERVATION: Education and the Pursuit of the Holy Grail*

- *LOCAL AUTONOMY*

- *PRECONDITION A: CHECKLIST*

Never tell people how to do things. Tell them what to do and you will be surprised at their ingenuity.

George Patton

OBSERVATION:

Education And The Pursuit Of The Holy Grail
(or why we need a process and not a product)

For years, we have been seeking the one universal answer, the Holy Grail, that will make all schools or all classrooms or all teachers successful.

Given the recent history of education in this country, it seems that we have found the answer time after time. In fact, just about every year we "find the answer." And with each new answer, we discard the old one.

We expect teachers and parents to mindlessly adopt each new discovery as *the* approach to making schools and classrooms successful. If they don't, we accuse them of being rigid and inflexible. We ridicule their unwillingness to change or try new things. Don't they understand that this time we have really found the answer?

The answer, of course, is that there is no one answer. The absolute for education is that there are no absolutes.[1]

There is no one way to structure schools or to teach—no one magic program for reading or math. There are only programs and structures that work in some schools but not necessarily all schools.

One common thread does run among successful schools. They believe they are special.[2] They believe that nobody can do things as well as they do.

They create their own special programs with their own special names. They convince their own special students and

---

[1] Except, of course, this absolute. Logicians will have a field day with this!

[2] Not to be confused with "Special Education Schools."

their own special communities that only their own special teachers can teach these special programs.

And maybe they're right. These special programs or curricula named SMART or STRETCH or ERSATZ don't transplant well. But at home, they are dynamite. At home they are something special.

Therefore, if there were one characteristic we could magically bestow on schools, it would be that feeling of "specialness."

Being special reflects a certain pride, self-esteem, and confidence: "Nobody can do it as we can." I've never seen a successful school that didn't openly exhibit this trait, but I have seen plenty of unsuccessful schools that didn't possess this feeling of specialness.

The question is: How do we get there from here? How do we foster "specialness" in schools that don't feel special?

One answer is to stop doing what we're doing. Stop taking bright ideas from school to school and expecting them to take hold. Instead, we must extract the concept of these successful programs and communicate the concepts rather than the programs.

Take algebra, for example. You read earlier of a program which embodied a concept. The concept was simple:

"Since high school success is highly contingent on success in algebra, we must design a system that ensures success for all students in algebra."

You then read of a program designed to make that happen. But it was *a* program, not *the* program. Once a school embraces the concept, it can design its own program. It could be designed hundreds of different ways:

- before-school, after-school classes;
- 10 minutes a day of algebra in history and French, P.E., and English;
- summer classes;
- night classes; or
- make algebra a graduation requirement.

The point is, the concept drives the program, not the other way around. Until the concept is embraced, the program, however designed, borrowed, or adapted, won't work.

There is a second piece to this puzzle. If making schools special required only understanding and embracing concepts, success would be right around the corner. But for a school to feel "special," its staff must also exhibit three fundamental states of mind: responsibility, belief, and empowerment.

> *Responsibility:* "It is our (staff) task to provide these students with the education they need."

> *Belief:* "We (staff) recognize that what we do can make the difference between students' success and failure."

> *Empowerment:* "We (staff) can make the changes necessary to make students successful."

Staffs so imbued create special schools filled with special people accomplishing special tasks in special ways.

The search for the Holy Grail ends when you look in your own schoolyard.

Man is not the creature of circumstances; circumstances are the creatures of men.

Benjamin Disraeli

PRECONDITION A: LOCAL AUTONOMY

Meaningful change in education occurs only at the school site. Schools, therefore, must have the autonomy and authority to make decisions in their own best interest. When the teacher closes his or her classroom door, autonomy exists. The only real way to change education is to change what goes on in that classroom. And the only way to generate change in these classrooms is to change the minds and hearts of teachers. And teachers will simply not accept new behaviors imposed upon them.

School-Based Management[1] has attempted to empower schools and subsequently teachers to make meaningful changes. Like most other movements in education, however, school-based management has often become an end in itself. Long hours and meetings have produced the "mechanics" of local autonomy, but in most instances, resulted only in a shifting of administrative authority from central office to the site. Principals and teachers learned to do the paperwork and make some of the budgetary decisions that the central offices heretofore handled, but the teaching–learning process remained virtually untouched.

Nonetheless, without a high degree of local autonomy, schools can't really change. Local autonomy is, therefore, a "precondition" for change.

We have found an effective means for assessing a school's current level of autonomy. The *Assessment of the School's Parameters of Authority* requires bringing central office

---

[1] A practical and definitive work on this subject is Dr. Richard Neal's *School-Based Management: A detailed guide for successful implementation,* National Education Service, Bloomington, Indiana, 1991.

administrators to meet with the principal and a school leadership team comprised of teachers and parents. Ideally, the meeting is chaired by the superintendent or a school board member.

The purpose of the meeting is simple: To determine the level of authority the school has in making changes in specific areas.

The question is:

Who is responsible for bringing about change?

And if we are going to hold someone responsible for bringing about this change, we must next ask:

Who has the authority to bring about this change?

Responsibility without authority is, of course, like beating a dead horse and expecting a good ride. Yet, in education, we seem to do this all the time; we expect the impossible and then wonder why it doesn't happen.

In an open forum then, you must determine where the authority truly rests—where the buck stops. And you must be specific in determining the school's latitude in each of the following areas:

Curriculum

Graduation Requirements

Instructional Techniques

Behavior Policy/Procedures

Attendance Policy/Procedures

Assignment of Teachers (Who Teaches What)

Hiring of Teachers

Dress Code for Students/Staff

Administrative Assignments/Structure Budget

Daily Schedule (When School Starts, etc.)

Bus/Cafeteria Schedule

Capital Purchases

Textbook Selection

Assignment of Classified Staff (Secretaries, Custodians, etc)

Assignment of Non-teaching Personnel (Psychologists, Nurses, Librarians, etc)

Maintenance of Grounds & Buildings

Naturally, local schools will add to and delete from such a list. But the point is to get everything out on the table. If the school thinks it can better serve its students by changing the curriculum, does it have the power to do so? If so, within what parameters or guidelines? Can schools request waivers of district or board policy?

What about the behavior code? Must the school stay within the guidelines of the school district? The state? May it become more stringent?

Can the school require more classtime or course work of its students? Less? Different configurations of the school day? School year?

These are thorny questions. Expect lengthy discussion. Begin with the goal of setting forth, in writing, the latitude your school has in each area. Define where the specific responsibility lies; remember:

If the absolute authority for determining curriculum (or anything else) rests solely with the central office...then the central office is absolutely and solely responsible if that curriculum doesn't work. The school cannot be held responsible...neither for the ineffective curriculum nor for changing it!

To change requires the empowerment to change. This is local autonomy.

PRECONDITION A: CHECKLIST

☐　Assess the school's parameters of authority

Precondition B:
Leadership Growth Potential

- *OBSERVATION: The Big "C"*

- *LEADERSHIP GROWTH POTENTIAL*

- *PRECONDITION B: CHECKLIST*

"Only those who dare to fail greatly can ever achieve greatly."

Robert Kennedy

OBSERVATION:

The Big "C"

I am often asked what one key ingredient is most important for the leader who wants to change a school. The literature on school reform is filled with books and articles citing the talents and skills necessary to bring about change. While I don't disagree with these scholarly journals, they generally forget the first and foremost attribute necessary. I'm speaking of plain, simple, gut-wrenching, confrontational, knee-knocking, bone-chilling, lay-it-on-the-line **Courage**.

You can take all of the interpersonal skills, group process strategies, and management information systems and toss them out the window if you don't have the Big "C."

Conversely, give me the leader with courage[1] and I'll show you someone who can overcome a thousand obstacles and still manage to move the change agenda. I'll show you someone with an accelerated learning rate, able to wolf down management treatises in a single gulp. More importantly, I'll show you someone who can adapt and utilize research at a moment's notice, applying theory to real life situations, making things happen, using whatever is out there to bring real change.

What are the implications of this Big "C" insight in the area of school reform? The first place I suggest we need to look is at the methods we use in selecting our educational leaders...our principals and superintendents.

Now here's how it really works. First, the applicants are "paper screened," that is, their résumés are reviewed until those with the top papers are selected for interviews. How does one

---

[1] There's nothing scarier to an adversary than the bold courage of his opponent's convictions--and let's face it, change, when it is initiated, is more adversarial than cooperative though we'd like to think otherwise.

get "screened in?" By having the best and most experience educationally and professionally.

So who do we get? The people who have done the most to make the system what it is today. The people who have played the game long enough and well enough to rise through the system. This provides us, unwittingly, with a sort of built-in guarantee, that the system as we now know it will survive with only minor alterations. Sure there are exceptions; good leaders do emerge through the system. But they are the exceptions, or latent mavericks, who suddenly surface as real change agents. Most school systems can't tolerate more than a handful of these at any given time. And the selection process ensures that they won't have to worry about it.

But wait; there's more to the selection process. For now that we've paper screened to the final (let's say ten) candidates, we're down to the interview process. Naturally, we must involve teachers, and parents, and central office administrators, and secretaries, and students, and the outgoing principal, and business and community leaders, and social workers, and local politicians, and community development representatives, and the union leadership, and...

Fourteen interviews later our winner emerges. And what basic prime attribute are we guaranteed he or she possesses?

This person is a GREAT interviewer...I mean, a GREAT interviewer! What did you expect?

In fact, over the last twenty years, through its selection process, schools have managed to raise the median interview skills level of its school leaders to phenomenal heights. At the drop of a hat, these people can discuss anything from the implications of the Middle East crisis on pre-school education to the impact of the drug culture on secondary school athletics.

But what's more, they can discuss these issues, and every other issue under the sun, without ever offending anyone, without ever taking a real posture. Years of experience and learning make these selected leaders capable of adapting their positions to the current direction of the wind. Not unlike their counterparts in the political arena, they have become adept at searching out the middle and the safe ground. Careful not to offend, they have become victims of the pragmatic survival cycle.

The cycle looks like this:

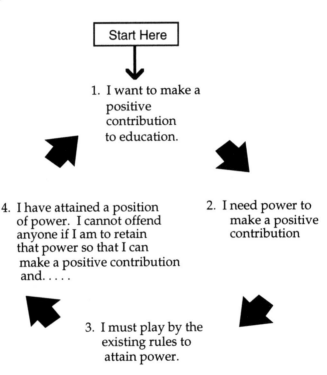

1. I want to make a
   positive
   contribution
   to education.

4. I have attained a position
   of power. I cannot offend
   anyone if I am to retain
   that power so that I can
   make a positive contribution
   and. . . . .

2. I need power to
   make a positive
   contribution

3. I must play by the
   existing rules to
   attain power.

In short, the requirements for attaining and retaining power compromise the individual's capacity to do anything meaningful with the power. We have created a system which, through the critical selection of leadership, perpetuates itself. This, of course, would be all right if the system were working; but it's not. Each day it fails thousands of children, betrays thousands of parents, and continues to raise false hopes among the poor and destitute.

But this system through which we select our leaders must share the blame. For the institutions responsible for passing on the skills necessary to run schools are also due credit for the current state of our schools.

The education departments of our colleges and universities must begin to encourage and demand bold innovative thinking, risk-taking, and action-oriented leaders rather than continuing to prepare school leaders for a repeat of the past. Most importantly, these institutions must somehow begin to engrain (because I really don't think you can teach it) the Big "C"...the concept of Courage.

I envision a practicum in which the potential school leader's performance is evaluated on the level of courage exhibited in boldly confronting critical issues, as well as actual results achieved. I foresee a certification ceremony where the dean gently places a sword on the shoulder of the successful candidate anointing him or her to the Holy Order of the Knights of Change.

I've heard that Lancelot was great against dragons but couldn't interview worth a hill of beans.

PRECONDITION B: LEADERSHIP GROWTH POTENTIAL

In our work with schools, we have learned (sometimes the hard way) that leadership is also a *sine qua non*. Leadership, (not to be confused with "management" or "administration") must exist in any school that seeks to change. In our early days, with an abundance of exuberance, we felt that we could find a way around this factor. After much subsequent heartache and confusion, we realized that we could not.

In schools where the leadership capacity of the principal is not developed to a point of moderate competence, change cannot occur. This does not mean that in order for a school to change there must be an "all star" at the helm. It simply means that leadership skills and capabilities must be developed or "developable" to the point where the principal cannot only manage the school but also lead the school in bringing about substantive change.

Prior to initiating work in a school, we complete a very comprehensive leadership assessment and profile. Some principals are threatened by such an assessment, others enjoy it. We explain to them, of course, that we are profiling "leadership potential" that is, the capability to lead if and when the system allows true leadership to occur. We find that there are principals in schools with great leadership potential who, like their counterparts in the classroom, have been stifled by the conditions which currently exist in schools and have been denied the opportunity to demonstrate the level of leadership they can provide. The *7 Steps to School Change* allows their leadership to shine through.

The diagnostic tool we have found most effective in assessing school leadership is the *Bass Multiphasic Leadership Inventory* developed and adapted for education by Springs Development Corporation.[1] The Bass survey administered to the principal and to a "site leadership team" of people who work closely with the principal provides a definitive and reliable profile in each of the areas of leadership. This, coupled with a working environment assessment, provides a sound basis for determining the principal's ability to lead change.

Through his research and review of hundreds of leadership studies, Bernard Bass, the subsequent editor of *Stogdill's Handbook on Leadership*, identified the basic components of leadership: charisma, individualized consideration, intellectual stimulation, inspiration, and positive reinforcement. These five skills must be enhanced and utilized on a consistent basis for a leader to be perceived as a leader. Management by exception, and laissez-faire leadership or an abdication of leadership responsibilities, are behaviors which must be avoided.

---

[1] Springs Development Corporation, Salt Lake City, Utah

The leadership profile, reflecting current levels of behavior in each of these areas, is coupled with an additional validating profile attained through interview with the principal. This provides an accurate assessment of strengths and weaknesses in each leadership area.

Leadership, like any other skill, can be developed. We subsequently enroll the principal in a one-on-one leadership development program to focus on areas in need of growth. A follow-up assessment is completed at the end of six months and again at one year. The objective is to foster personal growth. In most instances, this leadership development program is carried on simultaneously with the 7 Steps change process and does bring positive growth.

Some administrators balk at this initial attempt to identify weaknesses and/or classify principals. But it is a simple fact that if a school has a principal who cannot lead, that school is destined to maintain the status quo. No change is possible.

In a certain percentage of our schools (smaller than most would think), there are dysfunctional principals. While in rare instances a developmental program may produce some growth, more often, these circumstances indicate that there is a need for change in leadership. This need for change is typically reflected in the morale of these principals as well. They are asked to perform leadership and management tasks which they are not capable or suited to perform. This kind of pressure on a day-to-day basis generates a level of stress that is almost unbearable. In the long run, they benefit almost as much as the school from a change in job assignment.

Leadership has been identified time and again as the key ingredient in successful schools. "You can have bad schools with good principals, but never good schools with bad principals."

It remains, then, a vital ingredient or precondition for any school change process.

PRECONDITION B: CHECKLIST

❐ Create leadership growth profile of chief administrator(s)

Precondition C:
Staff Readiness

- *OBSERVATION: An Agricultural Solution to Teacher Burnout*

- *STAFF READINESS*

- *PRECONDITION C: CHECKLIST*

A mighty flame followeth a tiny spark.

Dante

OBSERVATION:

An Agricultural Solution To Teacher Burnout

When I first heard the term teacher burnout, I realized that where there was "burnout" there once had been a fire. Indeed, most teachers enter the profession dedicated to helping students. Only after years of struggling within an unworkable system do they begin to show signs of frustration. They become angry, cynical, and depressed; they certainly find little fulfillment in their jobs.

A few individuals can rise above this year after year. They manage to find within the system their own special niche and way of making a difference. These individuals are remarkable in that they face a tide running against them. Yet, they derive sufficient satisfaction from their jobs to maintain a high level of proficiency.

Many teachers, however, view their jobs as drudgery sustained toward an end: retirement. They endure as few hours as possible of this distasteful experience, arriving shortly before the first bell and exiting with the last. They hasten retirement by working through their unions to negotiate better compensation packages. They discourage their own children from teaching and look forward to the day when they can finally remove themselves from this abusive and demeaning environment.

Imagine being a teacher. First, you constantly hear that what you're doing doesn't work. Second, you're subjected to ongoing abuse by disrespectful children, demanding parents, authoritarian administrators, and manipulative school boards. The only out is summer vacation and ultimately retirement.

If, however, reorganizing a school's structure can help students to learn, it is equally true that redefining the teacher's role can make teaching not only more effective, but also more rewarding. Yet after all the research and debate, schools are still organized in the same way. One teacher and up to 35 students per classroom; it's neat, it's tidy, and it's the same way we've been doing it for ninety years. While this might have worked ninety years ago, it certainly doesn't work now—neither in terms of efficiency or effectiveness. Nor can it capitalize on available technology. Moreover, it does not allow teachers to fully utilize their talents in the classroom.

Because dealing with children on a daily basis is, even under the best of circumstances, trying and difficult (not to mention emotionally exhausting), it is imperative that teachers renew themselves. Only in this frame of mind can they bring their very best to the classroom.

In an ideal world, master teachers would teach four out of five years, and during the fifth year, be paid not to teach. Would that be an abuse of taxpayers' money?

Consider the following parallels.

We expect teachers to sustain an enthusiasm for learning, a deep concern for our children, and a willingness to continually give of themselves. Yet like the most fertile of farmlands, teachers lose their resiliency as their resources are expended year in and year out. Just as we vary crops from one year to the next, so we must protect a teacher's prime attributes—enthusiasm, vitality, zest for life and learning.

And just as we occasionally pay farmers not to plant, we should pay teachers not to teach after each successful, four-year stint. Let them take one year to do anything they wish: study, work for IBM, travel, enrich themselves. Once renewed and regenerated, they can return at their very best to our children.

Wouldn't this represent the ultimate pay raise—the equivalent of 25%—finally bringing teaching to a par with other professions? College professors teach 12-15 hours each week as compared with an elementary teacher's 30. Is it any wonder that some teachers can do little more than babysit.

The trade-off: this 25% across-the-board raise is in exchange for the elimination of tenure. Retain employee safeguards and keep politics out of the classroom; but get rid of tenure. The expense to school districts would be the same as hiring a replacement teacher for a year. Even this expense could be substantially reduced by replacing "student teachers" with "teacher interns." Teacher interns, like their counterparts in medicine, would work at subsistence pay for one year while practicing their profession.

Too high a price to pay? Maybe. But what costs do we ultimately bear when burned-out teachers drive students from classrooms and the pursuit of learning?[1] How much does it cost to support a burned-out teacher for the last 20 years of his or her career?

Pay now or pay later. In the end, it's a modest price to pay for good teachers.

—*Good teachers change people's lives.*

—*The problem is...so do bad ones.*

---

[1] In California it costs $34,000 to incarcerate one youth for one year; 71% of those incarcerated are school dropouts.

Nothing splendid has ever been achieved except by those who dared believe that something inside of them was superior to circumstance.

Bruce Barton

PRECONDITION C: STAFF READINESS

Staff readiness comprises two elements: staff dissatisfaction and staff working relationships.

The first can be summed up as a "gut level" understanding by staff that things need to improve. A truly satisfied teaching staff will not change regardless of outside pressure. Think of the shoe "pinching." Staff must be dissatisfied with the status quo. If there is no dissatisfaction—no "pinching" of the shoe—then there can be no motivation to change and change will not take place.

It is, therefore, extremely important to assess a staff's level of dissatisfaction. Because many teachers have found no way to really change the system, much dissatisfaction will be vented as frustration. That is, staff will convey a "what's the use?" attitude. While this attitude is disarming, it is far preferable to an attitude prevalent among the profession a few years ago:

Everything is going fine, it's just that kids aren't learning.

In such an environment change can't take place. On the other hand (and somewhat ironically), a high level of frustration is a strong indicator of the degree to which change can take place. The greater the level of frustration, the more potential for change.

To measure dissatisfaction, we assess staff attitudes through interviews and group meetings. We begin these sessions by setting out the hard data: test scores, the absentee rate, behavior referrals, the drop-out rate, graduation statistics, etc. Invite staff to respond. What do they think of these so-called "bottom line" measurements of their students? Is there room for improvement? Is there need for improvement? What do they really want for their kids? What would they like to see happening in this school?

Opinions, insight, frustrations flow. Again, over the past few years, staffs have become increasingly aware of the gap between what they would like to see occur versus what is actually occurring. This widening gap not only adds to their frustration, but also creates constant stress. Some staff even experience guilt; they believe they should be improving things but don't know what to do.

The second element of staff readiness also requires a subjective assessment. Our survey to initiate discussion in the area of staff working relationship asks whether there are shared values, a shared commitment, and a shared vision? Is there a common set of guiding principles which can be used as the operational basis for human interactions and decision making throughout the change process?

Typically, the answers to these questions are "no." In fact, they are so obviously "no" that we seldom need to formalize the obvious through a survey instrument. It is probably a rather natural outcome of our recent history in schools—the frustration, the isolation—that results in teachers and administrators functioning in their own worlds, laboring against the odds, with little hope or help on the horizon.

What we have are well-meaning people, each acting independently, each having little impact on the organization as a whole; and unknowingly, also acting at counter-purposes with one another. The typical school looks like this:

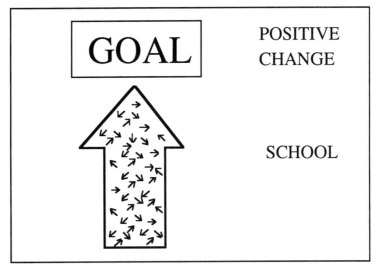

The school appears from its newsletters and public pronouncements to be pointed in the right direction, but the individuals within are moving in a variety of directions (again unknowingly) ensuring that the school will never get there.

In order to reach its destination, the school must look more like this:

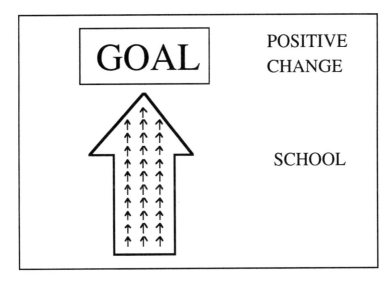

What is required is *alignment.* Alignment of purpose, alignment of values, alignment of goals, alignment of commitment.

Because this is so critical to each subsequent step of the change process, we ask schools to address this issue at the outset and, if necessary, set in motion an ongoing staff development program aimed at bringing about, and maintaining common alignment. These staff development programs can be carried on concurrently with the *7 Steps to School Change.*

PRECONDITION C: CHECKLIST

- ❐ Assess the level of staff dissatisfaction
- ❐ Assess and develop goal alignment and cooperative spirit among staff

III

THE 7 STEPS TO SCHOOL CHANGE

Purposeful, positive, and dramatic change does not happen by accident. It results from carefully planned and orchestrated activities. Those charged with running or operating our schools are concurrently being called upon to substantively change these operations. We often refer to this expectation as "trying to change the tire while the car is running."

Over the years, the process we have put together has come about through a combination of trial and error, happenstance, and sheer good fortune. The overriding criteria for adapting segments into the change process has always been "does it work?" And while at times these "steps" may appear unrelated and fragmented, in actuality, they are not.

Our experience has literally been a continuing learning process whereby we have come to realize, at certain junctures, that something was missing—some vital element that would facilitate change. And so, based upon this experience, we have searched out components and enhancements—from industry and education, from research and practice—and put together a comprehensive school change process...that really works!

It is a process that recognizes the need for everything from psychological adaptations to office automation. It is a process which understands that there currently exists within every school culture the seeds of the destruction of any good idea. It is a process which establishes the importance of leadership and the necessity for effective decision-making. And finally, it is a process which is purpose-driven, focusing on substantive change—changing the school's ethos—rather than quick fixes; and long term successes rather than immediate, superficial gains.

We call this process the *7 Steps to School Change*.

THE 7 STEPS

Through our experience in effecting change in a variety of schools at all levels, we have distilled into 7 steps the key ingredients of change. Terms and terminology may vary, but the substance contained in these steps represents a progression that all who bring about real change in schools go through.

1. **Create a "change" mindset.**
2. **Determine the method of scorekeeping**
3. **Establish a level playing field**
4. **Develop organizational readiness**
5. **Create a blueprint for change**
6. **Take action**
7. **Move to the next level**

In the following pages, we will explain briefly the key ingredients of each step. In some instances, we will suggest "enhancements" which may be helpful in moving through that particular step.

As you read, remember that all steps are not equal. Each depends on where you're coming from. Your school may have a great "change" mindset, but no developed method of scorekeeping; or it may have a level playing field (no discipline problems), but no inkling of how to create a blueprint for change. Thus, the need for enhancements in one area and not in another.

Some steps you will "complete" and move on, while others will require continual work throughout the process. And others, still, will need ongoing vigilance to ensure that they continue to lend the support necessary.

Finally, these steps provide direction; they are not a recipe. They tell you how to plug in the stove, turn it on, set the temperature gauge to guarantee that cooking will take place. But they don't tell you what to cook or what ingredients to add. Follow the directions, however, and you will learn how to find out what critical types of ingredients to add for your school. What to leave in, what to leave out.

The examples in this book—from algebra to athletics—come from real schools and real staffs who learned first how to bring about change, and subsequently determined what to change to turn their schools around.

Again, this is a Process; you and your school will determine what the product will be.

THE SEVEN STEPS TO SCHOOL CHANGE

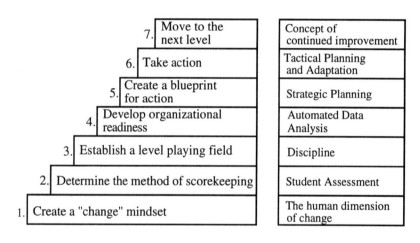

7.	Move to the next level	Concept of continued improvement
6.	Take action	Tactical Planning and Adaptation
5.	Create a blueprint for action	Strategic Planning
4.	Develop organizational readiness	Automated Data Analysis
3.	Establish a level playing field	Discipline
2.	Determine the method of scorekeeping	Student Assessment
1.	Create a "change" mindset	The human dimension of change

STEP 1

CREATE A "CHANGE" MINDSET

- *OBSERVATION: Football, Cheerleaders and Other Stuff That Matters*

- *CREATE A "CHANGE" MINDSET*

- *OBSERVATION: Football, Cheerleaders and Other Stuff That Matters (Continued): Everyman's (and Woman's) Junior Prom*

- *STEP 1 CHECKLIST*

Do you believe in Magic?

John Sebastian

OBSERVATION:

Football, Cheerleaders and Other Stuff That Matters

When I went to school, I played everything. If there was a team, I played on it. I never thought much about it, I just did it and accepted that as a part of my high school life. It wasn't until I was grown and had children of my own that I realized that there was another part to the playing field that I was unfamiliar with—it's called "the bench." My kids spent long hours on the bench. Like me, they worked hard in practice and put on their uniforms on Friday night. But unlike me, they never got their uniforms dirty.

When I became a high school principal, I saw more and more kids spend time on the bench, and I began to question why it had to be this way. If athletics were good for some kids, then why not for all kids—at least all kids who wanted to participate. How come only some get to play?

Then, one day I was asked to judge the competition for cheerleaders and songleaders. To my dismay, there were over thirty candidates and only eight slots. Twenty-two kids went home distraught, many of them in tears, after long hours of practice and work at fashioning uniforms, not to mention the hours spent daydreaming about leading the yells in front of the crowd.

And so, we began the "what if" thinking (always dangerous especially for those with any level of authority), and we fashioned the concept "what if"...there were a no-cut policy (everybody made the team) and what if everyone who made the team, played, and what if because we had an overload of kids who wanted to play, we created new teams, and what if we hired additional coaches, bought new uniforms, etc...what if every girl or guy who wanted to be a cheerleader, could be a cheerleader...what if?

Now some of this I had pioneered as a young maverick football coach. I had told the student body that if you go out for football, you're guaranteed to make the team, provided that you don't cut yourself due to missing practice or breaking team rules.

I also told them something else: I said, "Anybody who makes the team will be in the first game before the end of the first half, so it will be O.K. to invite your grandparents, and your aunts and your uncles, and your girlfriends and tell them to be in the stands watching for your number out on the field because you'll be there." I had no idea of the activity this would stimulate. The size of the team almost doubled. Kids came out of the woodwork, most of whom, I swore, had never seen a football before.

My assistant coaches almost buckled under the pressure. "How can we get these kids in before the end of the first half? They don't even know a shoulder pad from a thigh pad."

The administration wasn't really excited either. They said we had too many kids for the number of coaches...they said we didn't have enough uniforms, or pads, or helmets...they said football was for kids who could play football, not for everybody.

I remember presenting the football team at the first rally in the gymnasium. It looked like half of the stands emptied, a quarter of the student body stood there on the floor, calling themselves football players.

In the course of the first game, we had to exchange jerseys, and helmets, and a variety of other pads so that we could get kids in and out. Because I kind of enjoyed the symmetry of the whole adventure, I decided to start a kick-off team made up of kids who had never played football before. There they were, not one second of live football among them. My assistant coaches looked at me with those kinds of looks like "this had better work." I looked upward toward the sky and asked, ..."Make it work just one time."

As the whistle sounded, and the foot thumped the ball, our kids scrambled down the field with pads flapping and jerseys flying, screaming and shouting, arms and hands and legs and elbows flying everywhere. But they made the tackle, somehow they made the tackle. And that's all that counted, that's all that mattered...somehow they made the tackle. As the season wore on, I couldn't help but notice a very unique phenomenon.

In football, minutes of "game time" are worth hours of "practice time." In other words, every minute that a player spends in a game provides a tremendous learning experience, seared into his memory forever. On the practice field, kids tend to go through the motions; on the playing field, every ounce of their energy and concentration is involved in what's going on. As a result, learning is intense in those game minutes.

The phenomenon that intrigued me was that the game-time experience usually allotted to only a few players, now allotted to many, was providing the same benefits as far as learning to all of the players. Typically, on a high school football team, the athletes who are in the game more, will leave the bench jockeys way behind in skills and abilities. After a few games, there will become a great disparity between two left tackles, one who plays an entire game, and one does not play at all. As a result, the longer the season goes on, the more coaches are reluctant to play second and third stringers, because it brings about such a drop-off in the skills on the field.

With this team, however, it was different. The kids were proceeding along at close to the same rate. In fact, some young men, who would have absolutely been relegated to a bench position the day they walked on the field, were now actually deserving of some game time, performing far beyond our expectations. As a result, rather than having 15-20 ballplayers, we had closer to 40. This gave us a real stamina edge over everyone we played.

But more important, we had an enthusiasm edge. We had everybody excited about football. Everybody was a player. Anybody who wanted to could become a player. The resulting improvement in win-loss record, I believe, was more directly related to this fact than any other: if the kid wanted to play, he got to play, and the whole team liked that feeling.

I still like that feeling. It gives me chills just to remember the genuine excitement it generated. But I digress.

Back to being a principal. We did, in fact, institute a no-cut policy. We had to add teams, we had to add coaches, we had to find games for teams, busses for teams, it was a mad scramble. In basketball, we had what is called a black-top league, which is like a farm system, and anytime we needed someone to move up to a regular team, they would come from the blacktop league, which played everyday outside of the gym.

In short, we provided a place for everyone to play. Did it cost more money? Yes. Did we have more money? No. But we found more; and we found trade-offs and sponsors and donations and car washes. We found support throughout the community. Money (or lack thereof) is the quick excuse, the easy excuse, the all-purpose excuse for not doing those things that break with the norm.

And as far as cheerleaders, we decided that everyone who wanted to, could be a cheerleader, at least in their freshman year. A girl or guy had to try out, had to learn the yells, had to be willing to do some work. Then, we put them into groups or teams. Some cheering at one game, some at another. Some at football, some at cross-country, some at water polo, some selling programs at the varsity games; but all of them wore the uniforms and all of them participated, each and every one had at least one experience at being a high school cheerleader.

In some ways, this may sound immaterial. These activities don't have anything to do with academics or getting into college, or being successful in a profession (or do they?). But they do mean a great deal to young people. And if these activities are to be offered in a school, they should be offered in a way that is consistent with the overall good that the school is attempting to provide for each student. If athletics and activities are good for some, then they're good for all, and all kids should have a shot at them.

Once again, if you simply ask, "what if," you'll find that most things are possible in your school. You can have everyone who wants to, participate in athletics, cheerleading, songleading, and drama, and everything else. The key is that you must be willing to take strides away from the traditional, typical, old ways of doing things, and strike out boldly to find new and better ways for your school and for your kids.

A School Must Create A "Change" Mindset.

And not just in the serious academic pursuits, but in the other stuff—other stuff that matters—as well.

> Almost every significant breakthrough is the result of a courageous break with traditional ways of thinking.
>
> Nicholas Copernicus

STEP 1: CREATE A "CHANGE" MINDSET

There are two major obstacles to initiating school change. The first is the inability of those within the organization to believe that change is really possible. In truth, most of their experience reflects the opposite. The more things change, the more they stay the same; the more new programs that are tried each year the less difference these programs seem to make.

The second is that there is no real vision of how things could be different and no corresponding understanding of the underpinnings of organizational structure that must be impacted if substantive change is to occur.

One of the most important factors contributing to a belief that change is possible is the concept that "seeing is believing." Initially, we don't ask people to believe that change is possible—we simply ask them to suspend judgement until they are convinced. Then, recognizing that belief is essential to the change process, we carefully build in some early victories, or what we call "Impact" changes. If the school hasn't been painted for twenty years, we get it painted over the summer. Or if teachers haven't had a workroom, we make one, or convert one.

If parents never come to Back-to-School Night, we orchestrate the largest turnout ever seen. In other words, we focus our energy on an early and quick (but very observable) change.

I know you're probably thinking, "that's nice, but how can you achieve these things without money or resources?" That's the trick. But you can achieve anything you want, even without resources, if you provide sufficient focus and intensity.

Notice...I didn't say everything you want, I said anything. And I believe you truly can. The "algebra" example, as well as those later in this book, attest to that fact.

So, if you want to foster belief in change, you must make change happen. The quicker and the bigger, the better. Make this change happen by carefully selecting something that will make an impact. Then, recognizing how critical this "victory" is to the entire change process, focus your energy, creativity, talent, and whatever resources you can muster on making this happen.

One inner-city school, for example, focusing on "Parent Attendance at Back to School Night" jumped from a previous high of 80 parents to over 2,000 parents in attendance. No one believed it could be done, but they did it. The principal shared the pulpit with ministers all over the community on the Sundays preceding the event, exhorting parents to attend. Flyers and parent bulletins were distributed in supermarkets, gas stations, parks, and housing projects. Businesses got involved. It became the event of the city!

Did this change the school? No. Did it impact the education children receive? Maybe slightly.

But did it fuel the change process? Yes! It helped alter forever the hopeless belief that "change can't happen here;" it opened the hearts and minds of those involved with the school to the possibility of change.

This is a first and vitally important step. And it points out that the manager of change must become a master strategist in determining when and where to focus resources. Organizational change is not a helter-skelter activity. Rather, it is a carefully orchestrated and sequential scenario of activities in which current resources are developed in new and different arrangements to achieve new and different ends.

Nothing happens unless first a dream.

Carl Sandburg

CREATING THE VISION

Beyond understanding change is possible, staff and community must begin to understand that the old paradigms no longer suffice. In what we call Visioneering, we begin to explore breaking out of the old imposed boxes that schools have been confined within and moving toward different and more effective learning situations.

Schools and communities must concentrate on developing a vision of school; first from the perspective of the learner, second from the perspective of the teacher, third from the perspective of the community, and fourth from the perspective of the outside world in which the learner must eventually be prepared to function. All of this requires extensive work in breaking old thought patterns. During this step, constant effort must be made to focus on outcomes rather than the methods and the methodology; the *what* rather than the *how*.

The purpose of this exercise is not so much to create an exact vision, but rather to expand thought patterns. If this school really could change, what would it look like? It is, then, important for each constituency—teachers, parents, students community—to generate and share its own vision of how the school could look. We begin by asking each constituency to brainstorm five "What ifs...?"

...what if all students completed their homework...

...what if teachers could spend extra individual time with students who failed tests...

...what if parents had one contact person at the school who could keep them apprised of their student's progress in all areas...

...what if the pressure of time was eliminated and students had as much time to learn as they needed...

...what if...?

Creating a vision is an essential starting point. It opens the mind to the myriad possibilities that exist. When this experience is coupled with the realization that change is possible, a "Change" Mindset begins to form. Each subsequent change, or even contemplated change, will fan this spark as the community's school-paradigm begins to shift. Change is on the horizon!

THE MISSION

A mission differs from a vision. The vision is the "what" (what can be). The mission is the "why"—a statement of purpose. Once a change mindset has been established, it is important to revisit the mission. Most schools now have mission statements. These are typically lofty declarations of what all students should attain and bear little relation to reality. As a transition between Step 1 and Step 2, we recast this mission into the following format:

(Fill in the blanks)

1. The purpose of Lincoln High School is_____

2. To achieve this mission, Lincoln High School will _____

3. To measure progress toward achievement of this mission, the following assessments will be used: _____

Number 3 (above) moves us directly into Step 2—Determining A Method of Scorekeeping, or what the profession calls Assessment.

Most existing missions have little impact on the day-to-day operation of the school. The 7 Steps to School Change is designed to reverse this trend by establishing **systemic integrity**. This is simply applying the "purpose test" to every school action to ensure that it is consistent with and promotes the school's purpose or mission.

As a part of creating a change mindset, then, it is essential to culminate all activities by dusting off the old mission and viewing it from this new perspective.

There is one thing stronger than all the armies in the world; and that is an idea whose time has come.

Victor Hugo

OBSERVATION:

Football, Cheerleaders and Other Stuff That Matters (Continued): Everyman's (and Woman's) Junior Prom

If you've ever walked around a high school and listened to kids, you soon come to realize that high schools can be very cruel places. Social status as a student depends upon many intangibles. The bottomline: you're either in or you're out. If you're in, you have a wonderful time in high school. If you're out, you somehow endure the experience. It can tear your heart out to listen to the young people who experience pain and difficulty during these adolescent years.

One day, when I was a principal and my staff believed we could accomplish just about anything, we decided to see what we could do about one problem. It was Spring, passions were running high, and the junior prom was just a month away. Our junior class numbered about 450 students. As I talked to faculty sponsors of the event, I asked how many tickets were sold the previous year. I was told, "We sold 60 bids (couples tickets). That means we had over a hundred students attend the dance last year. Not bad, considering that in previous years the numbers went down to under 75."

"But it's the junior prom," I said. "Doesn't that mean that all juniors want to attend? What keeps them away?"

"One thing, it's the cost. Bids are cheap, but everything else is expensive. You're out $60-$70 on a tux, another $20-$30 on flowers, then there's dinner, and something after the dance. And for the girl, it's even worse: a new dress, new shoes, get your hair done..."

"But what if..?," I asked.

"...and that's not all. It's more than the money. If you're a girl, you need somebody who wants to take you. If you're a boy, you need somebody who wants to go with you. That can be tough."

As I walked back to my office, I kept thinking "What if...?"

The money angle was the easiest. We generated some funds from the tuxedo rental shops. The parents' club encouraged local florists to give special prices. We fenagled coupons for dinners and other bargains that helped cut down on costs.

No, money was not the problem. We were challenging social traditions that had evolved around this—and, I think, all—junior proms. Here's how we went about it.

Our school had two vice-principals, two deans, four counselors, and me. I brought us all together one day and announced a goal: 95% attendance at the junior prom. I then divided the junior class list by seven. Each person ended up with about 65 kids. "All right," I said, "each of us is responsible for getting 65 kids somehow, someway to the junior prom. I don't care how you do it. Become matchmakers, fixers, anything, but we're going to get them there."

As the next step, we spoke to the junior class en masse and told them we were going to make their junior prom the greatest in the school's history—and that meant getting everyone there. So we were changing some of the traditions and rules. You did not have to wear a tux, you could pick flowers from a garden, and more important, you did not have to be engaged or seriously attached to invite a person to the junior prom. This junior prom would be a fun opportunity for everyone to come together to have a good time. I put much of the responsibility on them. I said, "It's up to you to make this into something that you'll remember for the rest of your lives."

Naturally, we experienced a backlash from a small but powerful group of students (as well as parents) who would normally have attended[1]. We pressed our point. Everybody is going to the junior prom. I had my list of 65 kids. Each day I'd bump into 20 or 30 of them in the hall. Each time I'd ask who they were taking to the prom. I'd suggest names or set up dates. I'd call a boy and a girl into my office and say, "Come on, why don't you go to this together?" Sometimes it was easy, other times not. Some kids, I swore, would never break through the fear factor. Some didn't know how to dance; some didn't know how to dress, some didn't even understand the fundamentals of etiquette (like how to hold a fork or pull out a chair).

And so my counselors, administrators, and I gave lessons. We had kids dancing behind the closed doors of administrative offices. We showed boys how to tie ties and girls how to fix their hair.

---

[1] We were, of course, fooling with inviolate tradition here.

Understand that all this was above and beyond our educational assignments. But this was not only a fun diversion. It came close to being an obsession.

Daily I would consult with administrators and ask how they were doing. We built in a little team peer pressure. I would tell one administrator that his cohort was down to a list of 25 while I knew this administrator had 38 to go. As the concept took on a life of its own, support snowballed. Parents and community groups provided new ways for students to cut down on costs.

The net result: the largest, happiest, most excited group of young people to attend a junior prom in the history of the school. We had a 97% attendance rate. (The other 3% I believe did truly have some scheduling conflicts.)

The greatest challenge of the whole process was, of course, overcoming tradition and creating a new paradigm that people could promote. The most gratifying aspect of the entire undertaking was watching those students pile through the door. Two-thirds of them had never experienced anything like the prom and had assumed they never would—at least not in high school. Tall girls, short girls, overweight girls, skinny boys, those with blemished faces, the physically handicapped, the mentally handicapped, all of them—in one large group— dancing, laughing, shouting, having a great time.

Once again it had all started with a simple "What if?" It's amazing how fast barriers fall, and problems resolve when you venture forth and adopt a change mindset.

Are these types of endeavors important to schools, to education?

I believe they are. The school curriculum is not limited to classroom events. Learning occurs from the moment a child steps foot on the school yard. The learning isn't neatly packaged. It isn't segmented and categorized alphabetically by course title. Rather, it's mixed-up and jumbled in a becoming mind and a becoming body.

"Curriculum," then, consists of all that affects kids in their current state of "becoming." Proms, sports, and social interaction are important to schools because they are important to kids.

STEP 1 CHECKLIST

- ❐ Generate the belief that change is possible
- ❐ Create a vision

STEP 2

DETERMINE A METHOD OF SCOREKEEPING

- *OBSERVATION: The Basic Equation*

- *DETERMINE THE METHOD OF SCOREKEEPING*

- *INTRODUCING THE SUCCESSFUL STUDENT ASSESSMENT MODEL... S^2AM*

- *THE TEN CRITERIA USED TO DETERMINE SUCCESSFUL STUDENTS*

- *WEIGHTING THE CRITERIA*

- *USING S^2AM TO PROMOTE AND PLAN CHANGE*

- *STEP 2 CHECKLIST*

If parents, teachers, and other educators are really convinced that a good education is absolutely essential for all who live in modern society, then we must all search for the alterable variables and processes which can make a difference in the learning of children and youth in or out of the school.

Benjamin Bloom

OBSERVATION:

The Basic Equation

In our work with schools, we start with three basic premises:

- ❐ All children can learn
- ❐ Teachers can teach
- ❐ The school is the variable; that is, schools can change or vary how they operate to meet the needs of a particular group of children.

As I state these premises in the initial meetings with staff or parents, I'm greeted with nods of assent. Correct! Right on! Who could disagree with such statements of the obvious?

Yet, as I begin to explain what is happening in schools, they find that their school's actions belie these beliefs. The actions that the school takes as evidenced through its policies and procedures, its instruction and curriculum, its codes for kids and teachers, where and how it spends its time, energy, and money...attest dramatically (albeit between the lines) to the belief that many children can't learn, that many teachers can't teach, and that schools can't vary—they can't change.

To illustrate, let's construct a quasi-mathematical equation to depict our original premises:

Children + Teachers + School = Learning

Right? Isn't that how it's supposed to work? You bring children and teachers together in a school and learning is supposed to take place.

Now further, the way we define the learning components in the equation consistent with our basic premises looks like this:

❐ *All children can learn*: therefore "children" (short for "children capable of learning" in our equation) is a constant (K).[1]
Children = K

(The fact that all children can learn, (with the exception of some extremely neurologically handicapped) is a given. Research bears this out; it is not subject to change because of neighborhood, ethnic background, or any other extrinsic force or accident of nature. All children can learn. Period.)

❐ *Teachers can teach*: therefore "teachers" (short for "teachers capable of teaching" in our equation) is a constant (K).
Teachers = K

(In other words, put teachers in an acceptable learning environment and with relatively few exceptions, they can and will teach.)

❐ *The school is the variable.* Therefore the "school" (short for "schools capable of changing" in our equation) is the variable
Schools = V

(That is, the school can vary its operation, adapt to changing needs, individual learning styles, cultural differences, etc.)
Our equation then looks like this:

Children	+	*Teachers*	+	*School*	=	Learning
(All of whom can learn)		(Who can teach)		(That can change and adapt)		
(K)	+	(K)	+	(V)	=	Learning for all students

---

[1] We are using the mathematics symbol "K" throughout this observation to designate "constant."

We call the school the variable, because it is the school's task to change or vary how it operates in order to make sure that an optimum learning environment exists for these particular teachers and these particular kids. Maybe the children in this particular school come to us with no background in the alphabet; that's O.K. We can fix that. Maybe they come to us reading Time Magazine in the third grade; that's O.K. We can deal with that. Or maybe they speak a different language. We can handle that, too.

The point is, they can learn. It's the school's job to reshuffle its organization and procedures and adapt how it operates to meet the unique challenges or the special "conditions" that each child brings to school.

Sadly, in reality, however, the vast majority of the schools across the country function like this:

Children   +   Teachers   +   School   =   Learning
(Some   *(Some*   (That
who   who   *can't*
can   can   change
learn)   teach)   how it
                                 operates)

(V)   +   (V)   +   (K)   =   *Some*
                                              learning
                                              for *some*
                                              student

This equation, the real-life description of what actually happens in most of our schools (look around!), says that the kids and the teachers are the variables. And that as the kids and the teachers vary according to the children's ability to learn and the teachers' ability to teach, learning in the school will vary.

In other words, give me bright kids and good teachers and I'll show you some learning.

Take away my bright kids and replace them with kids off the street, kids from welfare households and crack neighborhoods, and there's not much the school can do. I'll show you little, if any, learning.

Or replace my good teachers with "bad" or "burned out" teachers and again the situation is hopeless.

As long as the real-life equation depicting how schools actually function looks like this:

Children   +   Teachers   +   School   =   ?

(Variable) +   (Variable) +   (Konstant)

...there's not much hope. Those schools which attract the "right" kids and/or "right" teachers, either through luck of the draw or the socioeconomics of neighborhoods, will be "good" schools where learning takes place. Other schools will continue to complain about their misfortune in being allocated low achievers—kids and/or teachers—in the variable factors of the equation.

Teachers will tell us how children have changed. They don't come to school prepared like they used to twenty years ago. They lack respect. They can't even speak the language. We're lucky to get them here, let alone teach them. Kids are a *variable*.

Parents will complain that teachers aren't committed to children like they used to be. They're more interested in job security, pay raises, and the list of union issues. Teachers are a *variable*.

Administrators will tell us they are doing all they can, and given the circumstances, the school's not doing all that badly...considering. The school is the *konstant*.

As long as we believe that kids and teachers are the variable, or more important, act out these beliefs in our day-today practices in schools, we have no power to change or improve schools. The future of education in this country is out of our hands. We are living out a deterministic philosophy of education. All that is left to know is what the makeup of the school population will be, and, sadly, we can then predict, quite accurately, how the children will perform.

In fact, statistics tell us that the best predictor of a child's school performance is socioeconomic background. We're left, then, with two alternatives: either abandon our idealism (and the research!) and admit that all children are not capable of learning; or abandon our current concept or picture of "school" and admit that it must substantively change how it operates if it is to meet the needs of children in the nineties and beyond.

Actually, there is a third choice. It is what we do now. Say one thing and do the other; claim that all children can learn, but then operate as if they cannot.

In the final analysis, we are stuck with the statistics. Affluent kids learn, poor kids don't.

This is scary stuff.

But hold on. If all children really can learn, then why don't they?

The answer can be traced to a simple but profound confusion of two basic terms inbred through our educational culture and broadly accepted on all levels of our society. The confusion rests on a false assumption that, narrowed to its basic tenet, reads like this:

KNOWLEDGE = INTELLIGENCE

This concept, though never actually stated, runs to the very fiber of our learning institutions. It runs through our system from kindergarten to the university. We need programs like Headstart, for example, to give pre-schoolers the knowledge necessary to be successful in kindergarten, and we need SAT knowledge tests to predict success potential in college. Please don't misunderstand, programs like Headstart achieve some outstanding results. They do so by simply accepting the reality that since you can't change the system, you had better prepare children to survive in the system.

For the reality is, enter first grade with all the intelligence necessary to learn but without the knowledge base and you're in trouble...maybe for life. Headstart figured this out years ago.

Take two children. Equal intelligence; that is, equal capacity to learn, assimilate, and use knowledge. One arrives home from school to *Newsweek* on the coffee table, computer in the family room, and college diplomas on the wall. The other watches *Lucy* reruns in the housing project waiting for Mom to come home from work. No books in the bookcase—no bookcase.

Predict the probability for success in school.

Remember: Equal intelligence; unequal knowledge base.

No contest. Schools reward knowledge. We only teach people who already know things.

But what if we said:

KNOWLEDGE = KNOWLEDGE, and...

... that's nice, but it's not everything and it's certainly not equivalent to one's intelligence, one's potential to learn.

More important, what if our schools acted like Knowledge only equals Knowledge and is more of an indicator of environment and experience than human potential?

If, then, all children can learn (and they can, as long as we don't confuse knowledge with intelligence) and teachers can teach (and they can as long as we don't put them in unworkable situations) then we have the opportunity (actually the responsibility) to make schools work. We must change how schools do business. We must make schools responsive to the individual needs of their clientele. And the exciting thing is, the school is a variable we can do something about!

Apple (Computers) had a product that worked. That was a konstant. There was a need in the marketplace; another konstant. But until they adapted the functioning of the product to the human condition of their clientele, their market was limited. Once they made their product user friendly, a variable they controlled, they suddenly created a huge demand for their product.

They did not, however, come upon this adaption readily. Relentless vision coupled with hard work eventually produced the "mouse" and the scaled down owner's manual that accompany the Macintosh.

Schools need to rethink how and why they do everything. They need to understand the corresponding impact every action and every decision has on student learning. They need to be responsive to each student in terms of knowledge and skills base. Apple didn't sit back and lament the fact that the general population did not have sufficient technological background to operate their computer. Apple changed how their computer operated.

If we truly believe that all children can learn, then we are the problem, and we must stop lamenting our fate and get about the task of fixing the problem. Successful companies take their clients and customers "where they find them" not where they want them to be (nor where they were years ago!). These companies can not change their clients (the customer is always right!) So they adapt, they change—they become the variable.

Because all children can learn we must find ways to make this happen in our schools. Schools must begin to truly operate as the variable.

Therein lies the life or death challenge for education and American society in the 90's. If we work it right, we can be there by the year 2000.

If you can't measure it, you can't manage it.

George Odiorne

STEP 2: DETERMINE THE METHOD OF SCOREKEEPING

How do you know where you want to go? How do you know when you're ahead and moving in the right direction or when you're off track and losing the battle? Educators today have difficulty defining where they want to go let alone assessing the degree to which they are getting there. Yet you can't track progress or evaluate the effects of change without a valid method of keeping score.

Before the kickoff in a football game, each team knows what success is. At the end of 60 minutes, each team can determine whether it has succeeded. We need this kind of honest, objective, and simple scorekeeping if we are to bring about real change in education. We need it for one simple reason:

Assessment Drives Change[1]

It is the bottomline, the outcome, the final score that sparks change.

We, therefore, propose a new method of keeping score—S^2AM—a simple and unique method for determining success or failure in your school. Before a school commits time, energy, and resources to change, it must know precisely what it wants to achieve. Test scores, absentee rates, and drop-out rates don't provide enough information. They are symptoms of success or failure, not outcomes. They provide a global perspective but give us no information about individual student success, which is what schools are supposed to be all about!

---

[1] I am indebted to Bartley Lagomarsino for this succinct and profound statement.

The Successful Student Assessment Model (S^{2}AM) offers a method for scorekeeping with a truly understandable format. It may be adapted at varying levels of sophistication. You may choose to merely adopt S^{2}AM's governing concept—school's measure their success one student at a time—or you may seek to fully operationalize its methodology. Regardless, there is much to be gained in shifting to this new paradigm.

If this method were adopted nationwide, one could quickly determine how well a school is doing and the extent to which a school grows and improves. The arguments about "good" and "bad" schools would cease.

INTRODUCING THE SUCCESSFUL STUDENT ASSESSMENT MODEL... S^{2}AM

Test scores... do they really make the difference? Schools concentrate efforts in raising standardized test results; still constituents remain skeptical. "It's the same old school," they say.

Why? A school is perceived as being "successful" not in terms of test scores or other statistical measurements, but in terms of its individual student success rate.

Think about it. When neighbors, or parents praise a school, they don't cite "test scores." They say quite simply, "It's a great school."

The implication is clear. It is a great school for students who go there because students who go there are successful. Period.

This is not to say good schools don't have good test scores. They usually do. Rather, it is to say that the simple concept that good test scores make good schools does not hold water, at least with the masses, i.e., the students, the teachers, and parents who attend and work to support these schools.

Now, educational leaders can assume that these people don't know what they're talking about and that in reality it is the test scores that make the difference; and, they can continue to aim for high test scores and improvements reflected on graphs and charts that show increases.

But, the masses do know what they are talking about. Good schools are good schools because the vast majority of students who attend them are successful. And their success goes way beyond test scores.

Historically, debate in education has given rise to two opposing themes in reference to rating schools; two variant viewpoints on how to keep score.

The first says that schools should keep score strictly by objective and standardized means such as test scores. When test scores go up, the school can rightly assume that students are learning more and that the school is successfully achieving its mission.

The other viewpoint asserts that schools are effective when students feel good about attending. Stress level is low, relationships are good, and students enjoy spending their days in educational pursuits.[1]

The problem with the latter point of view, of course, is that it admits to no real means of measurement for schools. The renewed interest in "back to the basics" in the early and mid-eighties and the resulting quest for concrete data have significantly diminished the number of proponents of this "soft data" point of view (though not completely eliminated it).

Supporters of the "hard data" test score method of scorekeeping, however, have not been completely successful in conveying their viewpoint. The general population is wary of standardized test scores. There are simply too many ways to manipulate conditions, or direct learning, to assume that increases in test scores equal success in schools.

---

[1]Admittedly, we've described the polar extremes and there are numerous gradations between these two viewpoints.

For example, a school may report…
…school test scores jumped 10 points!

TRADITIONAL ASSESSMENT

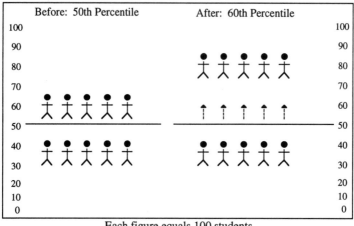

Each figure equals 100 students.

500 at 60	500 at 80
500 at 40	500 at 40

Note: The same number of students are failing….

or……school test scores jumped 10 points!

TRADITIONAL ASSESSMENT

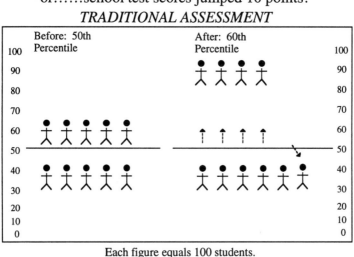

Each figure equals 100 students.

500 at 60	500 at 80
500 at 40	500 at 40

Note: Even more students are now failing!

What we are proposing is a new and much simpler way to keep score. It is based upon the seemingly self-evident principle that successful schools are those that create and develop successful students. This model, affectionately called S²AM, or the Successful Student Assessment Model, goes to the very heart of what schools are trying to measure:

How successful is each individual student?

A Dean Witter television commercial crackling in old black and white film depicts, I presume, the company's founder stating,

We measure our success one investor at a time.

In all honesty there is no other way to measure real success, and we are proposing that:

SCHOOLS MEASURE THEIR SUCCESS
ONE STUDENT AT A TIME

Again there is no other meaningful measurement; no other real way to keep score than looking at what students need from school and assessing whether they are getting it.

When a school can demonstrate that this year 60% of its children fall into the category of "successful student" while last year 50% fell into that category, that school can rightfully claim that it is making significant progress.

Further, if School A has a 70% successful student rate, while School B has a 60% successful student rate, then School A is clearly the better school. (We're not discussing how or why yet, just stating the obvious.)

And when a school begins to make strides and increase its number of successful students, all of its constituencies will know and recognize that the school is becoming a better place to be. There will be no need for promotional campaigns which depict 2 and 3 or 5 and 10 point gains in standardized test scores. Rather, (and trust me on this!) everyone in the community will know that the school is succeeding at a greater rate than it was previously.

"...an additional 10% of our students are now successful."

THE SUCCESSFUL STUDENT ASSESSMENT MODEL

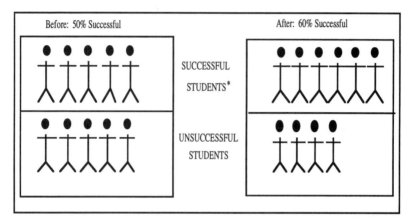

* See Successful Student Criteria

Do not confuse S^2AM with the "minimum competency" thrust prevalent a few years back. S^2AM rankings, as you will observe, do not represent minimums; rather they constitute genuine success.

Now, there is a problem with the Successful Student Assessment Model, and you've probably already guessed it. What constitutes a successful student? This, of course, given the nature of educational debate and debaters, could result in endless discourse. Indeed, there is value in such discourse, particularly at the local level. (More about this later.) However, for the sake of our model and in order to create a legitimate vehicle for comparison, we have broken out ten basic measurable criteria which can be used to define the successful student. This is not to imply that schools and school boards should not impose additional criteria which they believe, as well, are important in defining successful students in their system. Rather, our selection of these ten criteria represent a means whereby legitimate comparisons can be made between one school and another and between one year and the next in the same school.

THE TEN CRITERIA USED TO DETERMINE SUCCESSFUL STUDENTS

1. GRADES—With all of the concern and controversy surrounding the awarding of grades and the passing or failing of students, particularly at the secondary level, grades still remain strong indicators of how a student is doing. Therefore, grades must play a role in determining whether a student is successful.

Naturally, it is important that the school understand the criteria for specific grades and a "B" in English in one classroom correlate with a "B" in English in another classroom. It can be argued, of course, that grades can be distorted or highly subjective; nonetheless parents, students, and teachers (as well as colleges and universities) still consider grades a prime indicator of success. The value in using multiple criteria is that distortions in one area can be offset by others.

2. STANDARDIZED TEST SCORES—While standardized test scores cannot be the only measure, comparison of each student's knowledge to that of the general population, is important. The standardized scores in the S^2AM model are looked at in terms of each individual student rather than the school as a whole.

3. GROWTH ON STANDARDIZED TESTS—This is an extremely critical measurement, indicating, for example, that while a student has not reached grade level according to national norms, he or she may be progressing at a very rapid rate. The fourth grade student who between September and January "grows" in reading level from first grade to third grade is making tremendous strides, and while this student is not yet at the national norm, he or she is exhibiting accelerated growth. Significant gains in learning are taking place; these should be noted, applauded, and recorded.

Individual student growth is rarely considered, however, when judgements are made about schools. But, an inner city school which is bringing about rapid growth though still not yet reaching the norm of the suburbs may represent a far better example of a teaching and learning institution than the suburban school that simply maintains its level of academic prowess. This is the area where you separate real teaching from run-of-the-mill instruction. In elevating this concept of growth, schools can finally pay due tribute to the unheralded teacher who makes growth happen.

4. SKILLS MASTERY—The necessary skills in each grade level can be identified and a means for assessing a student's level can be (and in many cases has been) developed. A subset of the skills-mastery criteria, is, again, growth in skills mastery, wherein we are looking at acceleration in learning and attempting to reward the school which brings about this acceleration, while still recognizing that certain skill levels are necessary and must be attained.

5. CRITICAL THINKING LEVEL—Again, there are marketed tests which indicate a student's development and growth in critical thinking skills. Here again we suggest a subset for growth to offset low scores where great progress is being made and high scores where little growth is occurring.

6. CREATIVE THINKING SKILLS—Educators have finally come to realize that critical thinking skills and problem solving may contain elements of the creative process but are not in and of themselves measurements of the creative act. They must now begin to nurture and reward the creative process. Measurements can be developed from existing exploratory work in this area. Currently, many schools are working in the area of "teaching" creativity. However, the incentive to spend classtime on creative activities is diminished when faced with the reality that your success as a teacher or school will be measured only by results on standardized knowledge tests. Time to change all that!

7. *ATTENDANCE RECORD*—While this measurement seems mundane, attendance remains a strong indicator of how successful a student is in school as well as how successful the school is with the student. High levels of attendance indicate a cohesive community effort, a cooperative spirit between the home and the school, and that meaningful things are happening on a daily basis in the classrooms. The probability for success of a student whose attendance rate remains high is, indeed, increased.

8. *BEHAVIOR RECORD*—The behavior record indicates the extent to which the student is willing to submit to the basic social requirements of the school. While appropriate behavior, like attendance, is more of a precursor to learning, it nevertheless represents a necessary condition for learning to take place. Typically, problems in behavior have a serious negative impact on learning.

9. *ATTITUDE TOWARD LEARNING*—While assessing attitudes is at best a risky undertaking, it is important to have some type of assessment as to how the student feels about learning. Indicators in this area may include enthusiasm and extra work performed; willingness and eagerness to undertake new learning activities, etc. Because a positive attitude toward learning is so crucial to one's continuing and on-going education, it is important that it somehow be assessed. A combination of subjective reports such as currently exist on report cards may be a sufficient measure. For example, in addition to letter grades, most teachers now mark "Satisfactory," "Outstanding," or "Lack of Effort."

10. *ACCESS*—A summation of everything that occurs in the school on behalf of the student can be described in this one

word: Access. Access to the next grade; access to the accelerated curriculum; access to middle school or high school; access to the college and university. Access to the world of work. Access means that a student's skills, mastery, and intellectual capability are such that this student can proceed in accordance with his or her potential. Access means that a lack of education or a lack of required learning will not get in the way; access means there is no lack. It is the desired result; the outcome; manifest in an opportunity or chance given to the individual who is ready and prepared to move to the next step.

The criteria for determining access will vary drastically from grade to grade and from level to level. But specific criteria can be determined. At the conclusion of the fourth grade, for example, the fourth grader must have access to the fifth grade math curriculum. That is, he or she must be ready and capable of succeeding in fifth grade math. The eighth grader must have access to high school, not just physically, but in terms of probability of success.

No doubt some will balk at developing access criteria. In many ways, access criteria represents the sum total of all of the other criteria we have developed. It is important, however, to give it a crowning position as the culminating assessment in determining whether a student is successful. It also helps those of us in schools keep our eye on the ball. It is the school's bottom line.

S²AM: Successful Student Assessment Model

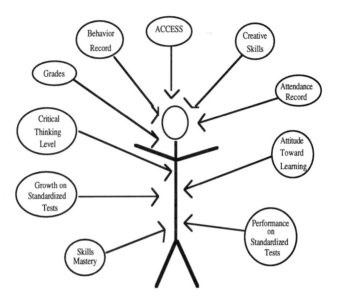

WEIGHTING THE CRITERIA

While we have identified what we believe are the major criteria for determining a successful student, we do not wish to imply that we have figured out all of the intricacies and ramifications. What you have before you is a multiple criteria, interactive, differentiated, value-weighted, combination of objective and subjective assessments.

But while the task of actually determining the level of each criteria (its interaction and its value, weight, etc.) may have been impossible twenty years ago, that is no longer the case. Any school can utilize inexpensive software to account for the interactive intricacies of these criteria. Individual student information generated from standardized test scores, attendance records, behavior records, etc. can be fed into the computer which will subsequently spew out a numerical success ranking for each student. That number will represent the summation of all of the criteria and will represent the relative success of each student.

To achieve this, schools need technology in two areas: first, to determine the relative weight for each criteria, taking into account its interactions, minimums and maximums, and synthesizing from these weights one meaningful score; and second, to provide a means for easy input and retrieval of this information.

Finally, without getting into the nuts and bolts of how criteria are generated, let us make a few general statements.

"All criteria are not equal."

Simply because there are ten criteria does not mean that each is worth ten percent in terms of determining the success of an individual student. Some criteria obviously must hold more weight than others. Without access, for example, many of the other criteria make little difference. Staffs and scholars must come together, and through some type of pairwise comparison, determine which of these criteria is most important, second most important, etc.

Next, some criteria can be rated on a numerical scale (for example, a zero to four scale), while other criteria might have certain levels—certain minimums.

But, think of it! Utilizing these criteria (after each has been reviewed and refined) the school can determine how many students are successful. And in making a determination it can truly measure the success of this institution called a school. The school can chart its growth as it pertains to real human success, and can analyze and adjust in those areas where instruction needs to improve.

This is scorekeeping for schools in the modern age. We call it S^2AM—Successful Student Assessment Model—Measuring Success One Student at a Time!

USING S²AM TO PROMOTE AND PLAN CHANGE

S²AM results provide the data for the school to generate a concrete plan to remediate specific areas. This plan begins with an assessment of "where the school is." Utilizing its clearly defined system of scorekeeping, the school assesses its current status. Once this is known, it can quickly determine "where it wants to be."

Point A represents where the school is; Point B represents where it wants to be; and the arrow represents the remediation plan, i.e., how it proposes to get there.

Now, suppose the school currently has 60% of its students who, according to criteria, are successful. The goal might be to move that number to 70% in this school year. The remediation plan represents the means by which the school proposes to get there.

It is obvious, however, that before the school can develop such a plan, it must determine why 40% of its students are unsuccessful. This is where the S²AM model helps again. The school can quickly determine what is keeping its students from being successful: test scores, grades, absence rates, attitudes toward learning, etc.

Next the school must address why students are not performing well in these areas. There are, of course, usually some obvious answers. But care should be taken not to jump to quick answers to complex questions. Poor performance on standardized tests, for example, may have its origin in areas seemingly far removed from test preparation or subject matter background.

Remember, the solution to a problem can only be as good as the identification of the causes of that problem. And since remediation plans are really solutions to multiple problems, correct diagnosis becomes critical.

Give this analysis the time and attention it deserves. Solving the "wrong problems" or directing energies to symptoms rather than causes can be a costly and frustrating endeavor. Problem diagnosis should not be taken lightly, because correcting the causes of the identifed problems becomes the essence of the remediation plan. For example, the root cause of poor performance in mathematics may be anything from problem solving, to arithmetic skills, or conceptual development.

Now, it's time to move, momentarily, to the other side and determine what the school has going for it. Look at the "assets" or resources and determine how they are currently begin deployed. This analysis, which can easily be depicted visually, shows what the school has to work with (people, dollars, facilities, etc.) and how it is currently deploying them (assignments and programs).

The trick is to alter the deployment of these resources to remedy the identified deficiencies. This is no small task, but it can be done. And once you establish this process of *assess and redeploy* it becomes the basis of the remediation cycle.[1]

In short, the assessment model must enable the school to pinpoint deficiencies. Whether the school elects to use the S^2AM model, a variation, or a more traditional approach, assessment is critical and must be established prior to embarking on change.

REMEMBER: ASSESSMENT DRIVES CHANGE

STEP 2 CHECKLIST

- ❐ Construct a meaningful assessment model
- ❐ Determine the instruments to be used
- ❐ Streamline the collection and reporting of data
- ❐ Use S^2AM to promote and plan change

---

[1] See "If All Children Can Learn, Why Can't All Children Learn Algebra?" This is a dramatic example of this redeployment of resources.

STEP 3

ESTABLISH A LEVEL PLAYING FIELD

- *OBSERVATION: Meet David Niceguy*
- *ESTABLISH A LEVEL PLAYING FIELD*
- *OBSERVATION: Behavior—The Perennial #1 Problem (or Symptom)*
- *INTRODUCING PROACTIVE DISCIPLINE*
    Building the Foundation
    The Concept of the "Social Contract"
    The Freeing of Resources
    Efficient Use of Time; Effective Enforcement of Rules
    Streamlined Rules
    Consequences
    A Numbers Game
    Types of Consequences
    Ensuring the Benefits
    Summary: Back to Lincoln High
- *OBSERVATION: The Only Game In Town*
- *STEP 3 CHECKLIST*

Schools aren't as good as they used to be, but they never were.

Will Rogers

OBSERVATION:

Meet David Niceguy...

Here we are at a typical Lincoln High School. Teacher David Niceguy, liked by the kids because he cares about them, appreciated by the parents because kids learn in his class, and revered by the administration because few discipline referrals emanate from his classroom, completes his course work at night through the local institution of higher learning and becomes certified to be a school administrator.

Somehow he weaves his way through the interview process and finds himself appointed as the new assistant principal of Lincoln High. David is excited. He views this as an opportunity to extend his influence beyond the classroom. His beliefs about kids and learning can now have a much broader impact.

David's peers are equally pleased. Finally, they say, we can get someone in there who understands the plight of the teacher. The students echo similar sentiments. They've known Mr. Niceguy as a genuinely caring and concerned teacher. He'll make a great assistant principal, they say.

Parents who have come in contact with him are surprised at the school's astute choice. Maybe they're getting their act together, they say.

David's principal meets with him during the summer. He outlines his assignment: all data processing and student scheduling; co-curricular activities along with evaluations of teachers in social studies, science, home ec. and P.E; oversee the guidance program; attendance; maintenance of the buildings and grounds; school liaison with the PTA...and, of course, handle discipline.

David anxiously prepares throughout the summer. He knows he'll be busy, but he welcomes the challenge. After all, here is the chance to put his beliefs and ideas about kids into practice.

Finally the first day of school arrives. On his way back from the opening assembly he's sharing some casual banter with students from his classes last year. He's interrupted by a red-faced and angry teacher who has just been hassled by three kids whom he confronted behind the field house sharing a joint (marijuana).

David listens intently as the teacher describes how he told them to accompany him to the office, and was told to "_____[1] off." The teacher knows one of the kids, Jason but could not identify the two girls with him.

David thanks the teacher for the information and assures him that he will "handle" it. Returning to his office, he brushes aside two phone calls from the central office, and his secretary's message that four teachers in the math wing need more desks, and grabs Jason's locator card. Jason is in English class.

This is too serious a violation to merely send for Jason, so he hustles down the hallway, finds Jason's classroom, locates Jason and escorts him back to the office.

Fortunately, he thinks, I had Jason in class last year; so this ought to be fairly easy.

Jason is indeed remorseful. Mr. Niceguy, he says, "I was wrong; I know that, and I'm sorry. But this school's lucky I'm even here at all. Last night my mother's boyfriend was drunk and busted her up pretty good. I had to call the cops. And after they took him, she got mad at me for calling the cops and I said screw this and spent the night in the car down by the levee. I barely got here at all."

David knows Jason. He knows the story is probably true. He knows he's a good kid. He feels for him.

---

[1] Fill in the blank with your community's typical rhetoric.

David also knows the rule. Possession and/or use of marijuana on campus: 1st offense—five days suspension, 2nd offense, transfer to alternative school (school for dopers).

"This'll cost you five days," David says.

"Oh, no," Jason cries, "gimme a break. My old lady'll blow up again... She said one more screw up in school and she'd have to put me back in Juvy...I can't take Juvenile Hall...I swear I'll take off where they'll never find me....

"Look, Mr. Niceguy, you know me from last year; you know all this stuff is true. You met my mother. You know you and I had a few hassles, but I never lied to you. I swear to God if you let me off I'll never touch another joint—or do anything else all year. I'll be a model student. C'mon, Mr. Niceguy...just one chance...I promise."

Mr. Niceguy, because he cares, because he knows Jason's plight, because he realizes the serious impact this will have on Jason's future, is deeply moved.

He weighs his options. He extracts the promise and commitment from Jason. He shakes the boy's one hand while the boy's other hand reaches to wipe the dampness from his reddened eyes. Mr. Niceguy hears the deep breath and sigh of relief as Jason turns to leave his office.

David feels a sudden surge as he realizes he now possesses the power to do good things for kids.

His surge is short-lived. In the lunchroom he is confronted by a group of agitated teachers who have already heard what happened. Grapevines work fast in schools.

Jason, they say, returned triumphantly to his English class making it known that he "got off." Between classes he also managed to stick his head in the classroom of the teacher who originally apprehended him, to let him know the good news.

Mr. Niceguy's day is further dimmed when at 4:30 the principal calls him into his office. Gently, the principal explains to David that this was not a good way to start. A group of teachers had dropped by after school to register their concern.

David goes home somewhat distraught but committed to clearing things up tomorrow. He makes a point of entering the coffee room where teachers gather before classes start. He makes his way over to the group he figures must have spoken to the principal.

He confronts the issue head on. He apologizes for any discomfort he might have caused them and then proceeds to give his explanation. He describes in detail Jason's home life, the impact a suspension could have on his future. He reads their faces. No sympathy. "If you could only have seen him in my office," he says.

"If you could only have seen him in my classroom!" the teacher says.

David closes by admitting that possibly he did make a mistake. That he was duped. But it won't happen again, he assures them. They nod. Sure.

David heads back to his office. Fuming. Somehow he's been had. He hardly has time to shuffle the papers on his desk when his chance for reprieve comes. The teacher is at his door with Lisa.

Lisa was one of the girls with Jason yesterday. He spotted her in the hall. Positive identification. All yours, Mr. Niceguy.

David questions Lisa. Yes, she was there; sure she took a few hits on the joint. So what.

"So what is a 5-day suspension," says Mr. Niceguy, "That's the rule."

"Not for Jason," says Lisa. "How come nothing happened to him?"

"We're not talking about Jason, we're talking about you."

"That's not fair," says Lisa.

"Fair has nothing to do with it," says Mr. Niceguy "Your outa here."

"Screw you," says Lisa, as she crumples up the suspension form, tosses it at David and walks out.

He sprints around his desk and escorts her to the attendance counter where arrangements are made to send her home.

On his way back to the office he thinks, this is how you've got to handle 'em. Tough job. But I'll get it done.

Mr. Niceguy is congratulated by his peers at lunch. Atta boy. At 4:00 p.m. he's surprised to find another note from the principal: Drop by his office before leaving. Probably wants to congratulate me, he thinks, as he straightens his papers and heads across the quad to the main office.

David is surprised. No congratulations—A petition:

The undersigned students of Mr. Murphy's 4th period English class hereby express their concern that Mr. David Niceguy, Assistant Principal, is unfair in his treatment of students. Those he likes he treats one way, those he dislikes he treats another way. *Unfair! Unfair! Unfair!*

David is dismayed. Driving home he tries to figure out how he got into this. Time will help. They'll see how consistent he can be.

Next morning in the coffee room teachers congratulate him and pat him on the back. Hold firm, they say. He vows he will.

His opportunity comes quickly. The teacher appears at his office door with Kelly. She is the other girl. He recognized her smoking a cigarette outside the girls' restroom.

The teacher leaves and Kelly sits down. Tears. She explains if her parents find out they'll kill her. She was only there because she and Jason feared Lisa was pregnant and were trying to advise her as to whether she should tell her parents about it, head for the clinic, or what. Just helping out a friend. And now this happens: Not fair!

Unmoved, Mr. Niceguy explains that life's not fair. The penalty stands, 5 days.

Kelly jumps up. "You hate girls," she says. "Jason got off, but me and Lisa have to pay—that's not fair," she says. "Maybe you have a thing about boys," she whispers just loud enough for Mr. Niceguy to hear before she slams the door.

The door reopens. Kelly sticks her head back in. "My father won't stand for this," she says through clenched teeth. "You'll see."

Not exactly a veiled threat. Back to the job. Four kids waiting on referrals from teachers.

Make that five. Two came to class without pencils. One rocking the desk in the back of the classroom, and one spitting in the hallway.

And number five. Pulled a knife on another kid behind the shop building.

"Have him wait until after the pencils."

Four o'clock and a call from the principal's secretary. Be right over. What this time?

Kelly's father called. An attorney—talked to the superintendent. Demands a personal meeting with the Board. Possibly a hearing. He knows his rights.

Time for the principal to step in. Time for strong action.

He calls Kelly's and Lisa's parents, apologizes, and rescinds the suspensions.

David Niceguy drives home in a fog. He moves through the next few days avoiding confrontation and conflict, immersing himself in routine matters.

But finally, by the day of the faculty meeting, he has it figured out. Standing in front of his former peers he explains the need for consistency in handling student behavior. He commits to providing such consistency…with their help. The rules will work, he explains; with just a few modifications…

"For one thing, the penalties for marijuana need to be adapted to the times. Instead of a '2 offense procedure' we're changing to a '3 offense procedure'…instead of a five day suspension on the first offense and transfer to alternative school on the second offense, we're changing to a warning on the first offense, 5 days on the second, and transfer on the third..."

"Now we can be consistent."

He reads the eyes of the staff. No comment. As they shuffle out to class, he overhears from one teacher to another:

"Don't count on me ever turning any student in; its a waste; I just won't see 'em anymore. You can count on that...I'll be consistent!"

In the weeks and months that follow, drug use on campus escalates. Other violations are also on the increase.

David Niceguy finds himself staying later and later to handle the discipline paperwork. His office is always crowded with violators during the school day. The more he works, the worse it seems the problem gets. The community is citing "lack of discipline" as a major problem at Lincoln High School. The teachers are no help and the kids are running wild.

"This isn't the way its supposed to be," reflects David Niceguy. "Maybe the kids are just getting worse."

"Why...I'm spending over 80% of my time on discipline..."

Certainly the names have been changed. And it's doubtful if our hero's ability to function would be completely compromised through one incident. But the scenario is accurate. Not only does it happen—it has happened in school after school across the country.

Because it is played out over a short definitive time period, what most of us see when we walk into the school is the resulting impact of the scenario rather than the scenario itself.

We see teachers unable to control kids, crying for support (and not getting it) from the administrators. We see parents who, at the mention of the school, call it loose and out of control, cite the drug use, lack of respect, vandalism, gang presence, or violence.

Kids, particularly at the secondary level, recite horror stories at the dinner table. Blatant cutting of classes, abuse of teachers, drug dealing in the back of the classroom, extortion in the restrooms ("You're lunch money or your life"); rule-breakers getting off scot-free. These stories are passed freely—student to student, parent to parent, business person to community leader—over back fences, at shopping centers, and Rotary meetings. One basic theme: "The school's running wild."

The school administration, in the meantime appears oblivious to the concern. The principal, in the face of this open hostility in the community, is out seeking help—but in unrelated areas. Usually in the form of more money: "We need more money for computers, or job training, or teacher workshops. We need new English textbooks; a new math curriculum."

Implicit in these requests is an acceptance of student behavior as it currently exists. Kids are different today. We do the best we can. No support from the home. The neighborhood has changed. We do the best we can.

Those administrators in charge of discipline, of course, are looking for a way out. "Serve my tenure as a bad guy and maybe I can escape to a curriculum job at the central office before my reputation is too tarnished. Another year and I'm outa here. Better update my resume. Nobody can really hold me responsible for this mess. Everybody knows there's really not much you can do about school discipline..."

Logical consequences are the scarecrows of fools and the beacons
of wise men

Thomas Henry Huxley

STEP 3: ESTABLISH A LEVEL PLAYING FIELD

On the surface, the subject of discipline seems somewhat
extraneous to what education is supposed to be about. Every
school has a behavior code, and some system and individual to
enforce that code. Can't we proceed immediately to the "higher"
areas, such as curriculum and instruction?

Unless a purposeful learning environment exists—an
environment in which teachers can teach and children can
learn—there is no sense in attempting any change. Until there is
mutual respect and a corresponding respect for the mutual
enterprise called learning, there is little hope of accomplishing
anything meaningful in the area of school change. In fact, most
changes in curriculum and instruction that are attempted in an
environment that is not conducive to learning, simply showcase
the inevitable. The inevitable, of course, is the feeling of
hopelessness and disillusionment as one watches well-intended
attempts at change fall by the wayside.

Each time we go into a school and talk to staff, the
curricular and instructional rhetoric quickly gives way to the
frustration centered around discipline. Ninety-one percent of the
schools we have worked with experienced behavior problems
which seriously impacted the instructional program. The fact is,
the best conceived plans to improve curriculum and instruction
will be rendered ineffective if a sound behavior program is not
in place.

A less known fact, however, is that effective behavior
programs are few and far between. They are not a matter of
simply putting together a number of rules and inserting them in

the handbook; on the contrary, discipline is a highly complex, involved, and interrelated part of the school program and must be treated as such.

It is so important that we've developed a separate change process for the development of a discipline program in schools. We call it ProActive Discipline. And, the time and energy a school spends developing ProActive Discipline pays high dividends.

Do not skip over this step simply because your school just adopted a new discipline policy or because things "don't seem too bad." Make sure you have an environment that can support the multiple changes you are about to introduce. Put it to the test. Ask teachers. Ask parents. Ask students...Ask David Niceguy...the odds are you have such a person at your school.

OBSERVATION:

Behavior—The Perennial Number-One Problem
(or Symptom)

Here's the typical cycle of blame: teachers complain that kids are out of control. Their behavior gets in the way of teaching. They complain that administrators don't take action, don't support them when they need it.

Administrators are overwhelmed by the sheer number of discipline referrals. Their time and energy are drained from the instructional program. After handling the day's discipline chores, they barely have time to complete the central office reports, let alone worry about what's going on in the classrooms.

Parents, from a global perspective, see their schools as overly permissive and "lacking in discipline." This is attested to each year in the annual Gallop Poll on educational issues. Discipline is always up there on top.

Many of these concerns, however, are reversed when the parent faces the specific instance of his or her child being involved in a behavior problem at the school. The parent, recognizing the flaws in the system, comes to the child's defense. The relationship between the parent and the school now becomes adversarial.

The school brings some of this on in the way it handles the mechanics of discipline, i.e., the way it notifies parents, and handles routine problems, coupled with the lack of ongoing communication, and even the less-than-professional forms, filled out in scribbled longhand by teachers and administrators.

Parents are generally not blameless, however. On the one hand they may have a rose-colored view of how their innocent babe operates in the classroom or on the playground. School administrators can count on hearing, "He told me the teacher's out to get him;" or "she never acts disrespectful at home;" or, better yet, "it's just the company he keeps—he's so easily influenced by others."

On the other hand, many parents of the 1990's are on overload. The job; trying to make ends meet; single parenthood; both parents working; tight schedule; and now the school says Matt's misbehaving. "I can't handle this!"

And then there are the students. They generally view the whole thing as unfair. They fan the fire at home by reporting that, "John did the same thing last week and nothing happened to him"; or "everybody does this, Mr. Smith just had it in for me."

The parent, in turn, responds to school officials saying, "I hear that half the kids on campus are doing drugs, my kid just got caught—what do you expect when you allow this to go on at your school—my kid never got in trouble until he came here—and besides, I thought schools were supposed to help kids, not punish them—sure he's got a little problem here, but kicking him out is no answer—how about some drug education program or something—and besides, if you kick him out, what am I supposed to do with him? I don't have time to deal with him—that's your job—that's why my taxes pay your salary— and another thing, I just checked your behavior policy and it says I am to be notified within 24 hours, and this is 28 hours—I demand my rights!"

Over and over from kindergarten through 12th grade these roles are played out daily in schools. Frustrated teachers, over-worked administrators, angry parents, and aggrieved students. The cost is enormous. Not just in dollars and cents, but in lost instructional time. And even more important, though subtly, in lost *morale*: Teachers who give up. Kids who learn to beat the system. Administrators who are overwhelmed and view their jobs as primarily dealing in negative experiences. And parents who lose respect for the school and cease to support it.

But there is another constituency, a forgotten constituency, who are the real losers.

It's the 80% of the kids, maybe yours and mine, who don't get into trouble. The 80% who receive diminished services from the school because of the time, energy, and resources spent trying to make an unworkable discipline policy work.

The kids who can't get in to see their counselor because the counselor is continually dealing with "crises." The student who makes the honor roll and never meets the principal. The children who innocently walk into an irate, or disenchanted, or burned-out fourth grade teacher's classroom, never quite understanding that she is that way because of a failed discipline process. (Maybe she's that way because some kid just cussed her out on the playground; or maybe she was the victim of non-support from the administration; maybe she just took heat from an irate parent; regardless—)

In a typical high school it looks like this:

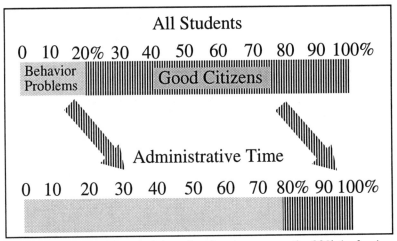

Eighty percent of the administrative time is spent on the 20% (or less) students who misbehave; 20% of the administrative time is spent on 80% of the well-behaved student body.

The feelings, the frustration, the helplessness described above is typical.

Who's wrong?

No one, really. With very few exceptions, we have well-meaning teachers, administrators, parents, and students.

What's wrong is the system!

INTRODUCING PROACTIVE DISCIPLINE

First, a few guiding statements which you need to know as you proceed into ProActive Discipline.

❏ *Nobody (least of all me!) said it was easy.*

It is a tough, sometimes lonely job, to put into practice on a day-to-day, case-by-case basis, what everyone initially buys off on "in principle." The concepts sound great. Applying them in the real world, without exceptions, is a difficult task. If you can't or won't support them, forget it; but don't try to fool anyone—especially yourself. Know that you're a part of the problem. This leads us to our second guiding statement:

❏ *If it were easy, somebody would already have done it!*

Take comfort in the fact that school behavior policies that work are few and far between. Making change in something as fundamental and universally felt in a school community as "discipline" will require all of the leadership, public relations, and human skills you can muster. Couple these with a strong sense of purpose and perseverance, and you have what it takes to achieve what others before you could not do. And finally, but most important:

❏ *It can be done!*

You—one person, a group of teachers, concerned administrators, dedicated parents, or dedicated students—can make it happen. ProActive Discipline does work. And when it does, the difficulties you've encountered, even the personal suffering you may have experienced, will be worth it—tenfold. You will have saved the lives—the futures—of thousands of young people who will pass through the hallways of your school for years to come. In disbelief you will look back and see how your actions impacted not only behavior, but instruction, curriculum, self-esteem of both students and staff, community support, and a variety of other seemingly unrelated areas. You will have made a difference.

BUILDING THE FOUNDATION

O.K. Let's begin. First, current behavior codes, policies and procedures, must be put aside allowing you to move forward with no preconceived notions, as well as no axes to grind.

Then call together a small group of teachers, administrators, and parents (and students at the secondary level). Selection of this group is, of course, critical. We could discuss at length the composition of this group. Let us simply say at this juncture that this group can be selected without concern for political allegiance. No need to make this a democratically constituted group representing all spectrums of thought and view points. Rather, you want movers and shakers. And you need people who are respected by their peers. Finally, you want individuals who will "hang tough" when the going gets tough.

Next, where do they start?

Quite simply, they start by deciding what they want.

A behavior policy that works?

A code that is firm but fair?

Rules that are understandable...?

No! That's not enough.

These are statements about the nature of codes or policies. But, in a school, discipline is a *means* to an end, not an end in itself. What we truly want in a school is:

> *An environment in which teachers can teach*
> *and children can learn.*

This is the starting point.

If, in the best of all worlds, we could achieve this without a discipline code, we would do so. But, before we're accused of moving off onto some esoteric plane, let me explain: this is a critical first step. Particularly for children. They must understand why we do what we do if they are to become supportive of what we do.

Just as important, we must continually return to our purpose if we are to establish a system of integrity. We must weigh each policy and procedure against our purpose to ensure system-wide or "systemic" integrity.

So the first premise is simple: establish what we want:

Premise #1: A school needs an optimum teaching-learning environment.

Steeped in experience, both in life and in education, we quickly cross that wide chasm to the corollary: Anarchy doesn't work. Civilizations, societies...and schools, do not exist in an ideal world.

People interacting together need parameters, they need rules. So in order to ensure the environment we want in schools, we need a discipline code. And further, we need one that works.

Premise #2: In order to ensure an optimum teaching/ learning environment, schools need rules.

Understanding discipline as a means to an end, we now return to existing policies. Upon examination, we find that in most schools these policies reflect those laws and rules that govern our societies. Statements of things you cannot do because they infringe upon the rights of others to live their lives as they see fit.

But schools are different. Schools exist for a specific purpose. A peaceful environment where everyone can go about one's own life as one sees fit is not enough for schools.

Schools exist so that instruction and learning can take place. The parameters and rules that govern schools must not only ensure a peaceful environment, they must ensure and even promote a *purposeful* environment.

How does a school go about doing this? First, by establishing the rights and responsibilities of each constituency. Before we can talk about rules and consequences, we must determine, consistent with the purpose of the school, what each participant in this enterprise has a right to expect, and what each is obligated to "pay" in return.

Some of the basics are the same as in society...on the streets. We can expect to be safe, not subject to undue intrusions on our personal freedom, private lives, etc.

But beyond these basics, we must establish those actions and behaviors which promote and protect the teaching/learning process.

Premise #3: In order to establish purposeful rules, the school must carefully delineate the rights and responsibilities of each constituent group.

Starting with students, the list might begin like this:

STUDENTS

Rights	*Responsibilities*
1. To attend a safe and orderly school.	1. To attend on a regular basis.
2. To be treated with respect by all students and school personnel.	2. To abide by all rules of behavior and conduct.
3. Receive instruction on a daily basis that is competent, well planned, geared to my individual needs.	3. To treat all persons, students and school personnel, with respect.
4. To receive the extra help necessary to overcome knowledge deficiencies or learning disabilities.	4. To make an honest effort to perform all classroom work assigned, i.e., to "try."
5. To receive ongoing assessments of progress.	5. Etc.
6. To receive personal guidance, encouragement and special assistance as necessary.	6. Etc.
7. Etc.	7. Etc.

And a parent list might begin like this:

PARENTS

Rights   *Responsibilities*

1. To be informed of my child's progress on an on-going basis.

2. To be involved in the planning of my child's educational career.

3. To have one contact person at the school, knowledgeable of my child's academic career, who can assist in resolving problems and concerns.

4. To receive special help for my child when he or she is having difficulty.

5. Etc.

1. To support the school's rules and student expectations.

2. To provide the time necessary at home to support my child's academic program.

3. To become a part of the school "community" willing to provide assistance in whatever ways possible.

4. Etc.

5. Etc.

A teacher list might begin like this:

TEACHERS

Rights	*Responsibilities*
1. To work in an environment conducive to teaching and learning.	1. To come to school prepared to teach all students regardless of their knowledge and background.
2. To receive the logistical support necessary to provide an optimum learning situation in the classroom.	2. To provide well-planned and well-conceived instruction each day.
3. To work with students who make an honest effort to learn.	3. To be empathetic to the needs, concerns, and problems of each student.
4. To receive support from parents in the teaching/ learning process.	4. To provide continual assessment data and feedback to the students and parents.
5. To have distractions from the classroom task kept to a absolute minimum.	5. To remain well-informed in my subject area(s)
6. Etc.	6. Etc.
7. Etc.	7. Etc.

In my experience, the best of these lists proceed from the very general (as cited above) to the very specific such as:

❒ Teachers will return all papers to students, corrected, with helpful suggestions, within 3 days.

❒ Parents will assign a specific time and place for homework to be completed and convey this information to the school.

Of course, the group we haven't mentioned yet is the administrators. Through ProActive Discipline, successful completion of the administration checklist is a strong indicator that the school is working.

Among administrators' responsibilities will be such listed duties as:

❒ To provide instructional and logistical support for the classroom teacher.

❒ To develop and maintain an educational plan for each student.

❒ To provide psychometric (testing) data to assist teachers in assessing student needs.

Nowhere will you find:

❒ To spend 80% of time on discipline.

This is because in the "administrators' rights" column, it will talk about the right to expect all students to comply with and support the rules.

THE CONCEPT OF THE "SOCIAL CONTRACT"

Once a school community has formulated, endorsed, and embraced the rights and responsibilities of the constituencies, it has, in essence created a type of social contract. This concept is critical to ProActive Discipline. To each constituency, it says:

To be a part of this community, and to be a recipient of its benefits, you are required to act and perform in this way.

Some school staffs like to take this concept and run with it. "We have the right to expect that parents will...and that students will...hallelujah!"

Caution: All contracts have two sides. Give and take.

Let's take a look at the student's side. The student who fulfills his or her responsibilities...comes to class, tries, completes assignments, lives within the rules...this student has a right to an education; well-planned classes, dedicated, creative teaching, updated curriculum, and genuine concern for his/her strengths and weaknesses.

Don't be confused. I'm not just talking about the kid who gets "A's" and scores at the top in statewide tests.

That's not what the agreement says. It says if I'm fulfilling my responsibilities in respect to the rules, effort, attendance, etc., then I have a right to an education. It doesn't say anything about my educational background, my homelife, my knowledge, or skills...or my native language.

This contract says that I have a right to an education even if I've been a dropout for two years, read at the 3rd grade level in 7th grade, and go home to a drug-infested neighborhood.

Of course, a school could circumvent its responsibilities to such students. It could say that kids have a right to an education if they are at grade level in skills and knowledge, and if they have attended school regularly since kindergarten, and if they are proficient in English—. But nobody signs one-sided contracts. And this effort to "stack the deck" to protect the staff, will kill the deal and we'll be back to square one.

So *all* kids have these rights provided they shoulder their responsibilities. This looks good on paper, but it's scary stuff to those who have been in real schools.

How can a school possibly take care of such a diverse population. How can it expect to educate kids when they come with such variance in knowledge and skill levels?

Where does the school get the resources—the money—the time—the people?

The answer is simple. The school already has the resources. But it chooses to spend them on discipline. Now taking everything thus far at face value and not just as an exercise on paper, the school's challenge is to convert these resources from discipline to instruction and learning.

This is really getting scary! You see, we know how to work discipline (not make it work, but work at making it not work) but we know little about working instruction and learning. And we know even less about creating schools where everybody learns.

In short, it is much easier (and safer) at this juncture to do what most schools have always done: consider the foregoing—the committee, the establishment of purpose, the rights and responsibilities—as an interesting exercise and then revert quietly to the old ways.

Stop and think: is your school willing to accept this challenge—this trailblazing into the unknown?

Again, implicit in the social contract is the expectation that complying students will receive a fair allocation of the administrative and instructional resources necessary to support their educational needs.

In other words, you need to take the administrative and instructional resources—time, money, energy—spent on discipline (80% remember?) and put them toward the education of the average, complying student.

You need to spend these resources educating the 80% instead of disciplining the 20%.

This is critical, for as long as you continue to short change complying students, your school will not work.

In effect, you say to these kids, "Pay for $8.00 worth of services and we'll give you $2.00 worth; we've got to use your other $6.00 worth on the kids who won't pay."

The cycle is vicious...

...because you don't provide complying students with the education they deserve, you have fewer and fewer complying students.

...because you have fewer and fewer complying students, you have to spend more resources on the non-complying students.

...this leaves you with less to spend on complying students which moves you even farther from providing the education they deserve; which results in fewer and fewer complying students... etc. etc.

Let us repeat, this concept of the social contract—rights and responsibilities—looks great on paper, but in reality it has a half-life of about 2 NANO seconds, unless it is put into place as part of an overall system designed to support it.

Let's take a look at how we put that system together.

THE FREEING OF RESOURCES

Thus far you've convened your constituencies, developed an understanding of the purpose of student discipline, and delineated the rights and responsibilities of each group. Now this is where the tire meets the road. How do you create a system to make this really happen?

You start by viewing the administrative workload in an entirely different manner. For simplicity's sake, we'll talk about that one resource most adaptable to changing needs: time.

David Niceguy's workday can be referred to as "100% of his time." Now, we saw him attempt to increase this as the discipline demands increased and he worked later hours. But we also observed that extending his workday had little real impact on his ability to get the job done. So, for our purposes, let's keep him at the 100% level.

In assessing where his time went, David determined that 80% of it was going toward discipline. If he had gone a step further, he would have determined that this 80% of his time was indeed being spent on 20% (probably less) of the student population.

David's response to pressure was, quite naturally, reactionary; that is, as the pressure of discipline became greater, he reacted and adjusted his time accordingly.

He really had only two choices. Either adapt (increase) his schedule or simply let discipline go. Don't handle it. Deal with the kids he had time for and forget the rest. Not a good alternative. The school comes apart at the seams, not unlike in our other scenario, only faster. Some kids get sent to the office and they get off scot-free—nobody even sees them—because of work overload.

So David chose the more honorable route: expand the percentage of time he spent on discipline. David never considered changing the system. The system was beyond his scope of control. It was a konstant, not a variable. The only variables David perceived he had to work with were "time" and "energy." Work more...and harder.

But what if...

What if, in David's school, a group such as we've described had established their purpose, formulated a statement of rights, and responsibilities, and was ready to put the meat on the bone—establish the policies, procedures, rules, and codes which would make it all happen.

And what if, up front, that group established a guiding principle that read something like this:

While every effort must be made to ensure that each rule is fair, and will be fairly applied; we must also strive to streamline the application of these rules to ensure that the school administration spends no more than 20% of its time in the apprehension and servicing of those who choose to break the rules. This will ensure that the vast majority of the administration's time is spent providing educational services for the vast majority of the students who comply with the rules and fulfill their responsibilities as students.

In other words, you don't just want rules that work, you want rules that can be "worked" (administered) efficiently. You must protect the administration's prime resource—time.

EFFICIENT USE OF TIME; EFFECTIVE ENFORCEMENT OF RULES

In writing the rules and establishing the procedures and consequences, then, the committee must keep its eye on the general student body—those who fulfill their contracted obligations—rather than on the rule-breakers.

Procedures and consequences must be designed to:

1. Protect each student's right to an optimum education; this includes ensuring that complying students are not penalized with less than adequate instruction due to lack of administrative support for these classes...due to lack of administrative time...due to excessive time spent on discipline.

2. Motivate students "on the fence" to comply with the rules by making the consequences for inappropriate behavior stringent and (this is really important!) the educational and co-educational program attractive enough so that students will want to reap the benefits.

3. Motivate the transgressors to change their ways; again, through the application of stringent consequences and the attractiveness of the educational and co-educational programs provided to complying students.

Putting this all together, then, what do our rules, consequences, and procedures look like?

STREAMLINED RULES

First the rules. They must be simple, straightforward, understandable and...

...each rule must be written as a compound statement.

Why?

Because.

Because each rule must have a "because" in the middle.

What better way for kids to understand why you have a rule? What better way to instill the purpose of each rule? And what better way, in formulating rules, to force compliance with the "purpose" principle established earlier. (You need rules so that teaching and learning can take place.)

We call these *conjunctive* rules. First because they contain the conjunction "because"; and second, because they "con-join" each rule with the purpose of the rules.

When you apply the "purpose test" to a rule, you allow students insight into the rationale for the rule. You cease to be lawgivers, authorities who know what's best for everyone, and become lawmakers creating understandable rules designed to achieve a specific purpose.

No longer can the rule read:

"Students may not chew gum."

Now it must read:

"Students may not chew gum because...."

And the because must relate to the purpose of the school—learning and instruction—otherwise the rule does not pass the "purpose test" and it can't be a part of the discipline code.

All rules must pass the purpose test. They must have a "because" which is understandable to kids. They must be conjunctive rules containing the conjunction "because" which conjoins the rule to the purpose.

Students may not agree with the rationale behind every rule. That's all right. What they will understand is that the school is acting in a discernible, purposeful way; and, that the school is acting in their best interest, to protect the environment necessary for their growth.

Couple this way of thinking with a school program that is really working—that aggressively seeks to take students from where they are, and move them, academically, to where they need to be—and you have the makings of a system that works.

When kids understand why the rules exist and simultaneously feel the benefits of the existence of the rules, they will, in turn, support the rules...

... which in turn reinforces the rules...

But, if you're going to have a rule against gum chewing, you'd better figure out how gum chewing negatively impacts the instructional program, or forget the rule:

> Students may not chew gum because the chewing and popping of gum distracts the teacher when presenting material to students.

or

...because the mess left behind (under desks and chairs, on the floor) requires custodial time for cleanup which could be spent on more productive, instruction–related needs.

How about fighting on campus—drugs, alcohol, tardies, class cuts, defiance, disrespect. Can you relate the impact of these offenses to the instructional program? Sure. And when you do, you'll have rules that make sense; that can be defended and most important, that promote the instructional purpose of the school.

Some "becauses" will relate directly to administrative and teacher time. This is all right as long as students can see how this time is put to use for their benefit:

> *Tardiness cannot be tolerated because it requires teachers and administrators to spend time and energy keeping records and disciplining tardy students rather than working with students individually between classes and after school.*

CONSEQUENCES

Now, step two. The consequences

It's a numbers game, no doubt about it. A thousand kids and three administrators, 2500 kids and six administrators...it all equals trouble.

The fact is that the odds are on the perpetrator's side; the odds are that if the student does it—tries it—breaks the rule— he or she won't get caught. That's reality, and kids know the odds. The street teaches probability and kids are ardent learners.

Let's face it, the adults are outnumbered. Too many nooks and crannies to hide in, to pass drugs in; impossible task to patrol a campus. Schools can, of course, hire security guards; and more security guards; and more security guards...[1]

Put barbed wire on the fence tops; observation towers at each corner of the campus.

---

[1] Security guards serve a vital purpose in many schools. But that purpose is to keep the rest of the world (those who are not a part of the social contract) out.

Wait a minute. I thought this was a school. A place with a purpose.

"Sure, but you can't let them go around breaking the rules. Send the administrators out—have them patrol the campus. Put teachers on hall duty in their spare time...." It won't work.

Where's the problem?

Assuming you've done the ground work: established the purpose; developed the social contract, the rights and responsibilities; and devised purposeful rules, the problem inevitably lies in the consequences.

Well-meaning, humane educators, in an unwitting attempt to help and counsel students who break rules, in fact, accomplish just the opposite.

Rather than reforming the rule violators, schools have succeeded in creating whole student bodies of risk-taking rule breakers.

When it comes to assessing the probability of their own well-being, kids, regardless of their math competence, can compute effectively, thank you. They know that the ratio of students to administrators is 300 or 400 or 500 to one. And they know, also, that these administrators are tremendously over-worked, reacting to demands from everyone.

Then you add the capper. The consequences. A student can say: "All right, I'll light up this joint; the odds are I won't get caught; but even if I *do* get caught, it's only my first offense; on your first offense all you get is a 'parent conference' or maybe a 2-day suspension... take a chance!"

And they do. And they're right about the odds; they probably won't get caught.

Unfortunately, this pattern of thinking extends far beyond the small segment of individuals who will typically take irrational risks to participate in antisocial behavior. We're not talking about the criminal mind here, the psychopath who will risk severe consequences. Schools have made the risk so small that the average kid—the student body at large—can give it a try with little worry about getting caught.

Schools, in effect, have made it "safe" to break the rules through these well-meaning slap-on-the-wrist consequences.

A NUMBERS GAME

And the safer schools make it, the greater the peer pressure to take a chance which eventually spirals the school "out-of-control."

A particular elementary school, for example, states in its behavior code that a child will be suspended on his/her seventh serious violation. Such serious violations include fighting, verbal abuse of teachers, classroom disruption, etc.

There are 600 students in this school. Now let's take a look at this. That means, theoretically, that there could be 600 X 6 = 3,600 serious violations before any students was ever suspended.

Now, of course, many students will never get to six violations, so the number 3,600 appears inflated.

Take no comfort. Remember the administrator to student ratio? In this school, it happens to be 600 students to one administrator. The odds are, then, that many violations will simply go undetected. Kids won't get caught.

So in reality, we're talking about suspension on the 7th *apprehension*, rather than the 7th *violation*. It would be extremely rare for a student to be apprehended each time he or she violates a rule. Children are too smart. A conservative estimate might be that a child would violate the rules 30 times and get caught 6. This 5:1 ratio can swell as the school spirals out of control.

So let's say, conservatively, that 20% (120 students) of the 600 students in our elementary school are rule violators. And that in order to be caught six times, they had violated the rules

30 times. That means that 120 students x 30 violations = 3,600 violations. Same number as above!

And this does not take into account the scattering of violations among the other 80% of the student population who are surely influenced to cross over the line because rule infractions are so abundant, and rule breaking is such a "safe" endeavor.

The result? A school out of control. A principal spending 80% of her time on discipline; frustrated and abused teachers pulling their hair out; little administrative support for instruction; dissatisfied parents; and kids running wild, when in actuality, they would prefer a more orderly, purposeful, supportive environment.

Why? Well-meaning adults, concerned about the impact of serious consequences on young minds, who withhold or water-down consequences fearing that these children will be lost forever.

In fact, we are losing many of the children...and maybe forever.

The answer?

Honest, straightforward consequences that serve as a deterrent to risk-taking.

TYPES OF CONSEQUENCES

There are two types of deterrents: specific and general. The former asks the question, "What will it take to ensure that this individual will not behave in this manner again?" This works well with a student body of one. With one student in your school (or one child in your family), you can say, "Maybe a serious warning is all it will take; maybe a note home."

With student bodies of more than one, however, it's different. You must look to the general deterrent. "What will it take to ensure that the general student population refrains from this behavior?

In asking this question, you must also add:

"…given the fact that the ratio of students to administrators is 500-1…

and…

"…given the fact that we want 80% of our administrator's time supporting the instructional program, rather than controlling behavior…"

In short, the penalty must be great enough to discourage risk-taking. This is not a matter of vindictiveness, or vengeance. The school is simply establishing consequences which act as a true deterrent to rule breaking.

The child must say:

"Sure, the odds are I'll get away with it…but it's not worth taking the chance…'cause if I do get caught…!"

Some will call this inhumane. Because in order to make this system work, the consequences will have to be strictly enforced, and this means that a few kids will try the system, will get caught, and will receive harsh consequences. Detractors will call these students "scapegoats" and demand that the system be changed.

I submit otherwise. Behavior codes that exist now in schools are, in the long run, much more inhumane.

Right now most schools' consequences encourage vast numbers of middle-of-the-road, fence sitters, to take chances, get involved in antisocial, illegal, and self-destructive activities; we take taxpayers money, and under the pretense of "education," create environments in which teachers can't teach and kids can't learn, and this includes the vast majority—the 80% who are good citizens.

But, there is a way to make this the most humane/child-nurturing system ever.

Unfortunately, however, too many schools stop here. A few see ProActive Discipline and its seemingly stringent consequences as too authoritarian and Draconian to even consider.

Others make an even worse mistake. They quickly see the logic of the system and immediately seek to put it into place. They throw out the old—the laissez-faire rules and consequences—and replace them with a hard-nosed crunch approach shortcutting through the developmental process and ignoring the common understanding necessary to evolve the new system.

It won't work that way either. Behavior and discipline codes are not simply one independent element in the school system which can be reviewed, restructured, and then replaced into the existing system. Rather, the behavior code is an integrated interdependent function that supports and is supported by the entire program at the school.

You can't skip the social contract step or the understanding of purpose and simply make the consequences stiffer. Adjusting the discipline policy alone usually causes chaos, polarization and eventual breakdown of the entire behavior system.

It takes more...read on.

ENSURING THE BENEFITS

Remember developing the concept of discipline as a "means to an end?" Well, when you talk about changing behavior policies, you must also consider the impact that resulting positive changes in student behavior will have on the "end," i.e., instruction and learning.

It is naive to think that you can "sell" changes in a behavior code to students or to parents exclusively on the promise that it will make children better citizens, more polite or respectful. But, while it is a fact that inept discipline codes have resulted in intolerable behavior in schools, it is just as true that this intolerable behavior has, in turn, forced us to accept some intolerable instruction in our classrooms.

Now, here's the catch. And coming full circle, here's the payoff—the reward for students—and parents. If you change the behavior code, which, in turn, dramatically improves student behavior; and if administrators can now spend 80% of their time supporting instruction; and if teachers subsequently are free to teach and plan and work with students on learning rather than behavior, then you ought to have...

...No, you ought to expect...No, you ought to demand...better, more exciting, more creative, more productive, more student–centered, more individualized, more dynamic, more focused...

...*INSTRUCTION!*

That's how it works! There must be a payoff or it won't work. With a payoff, it can't miss!

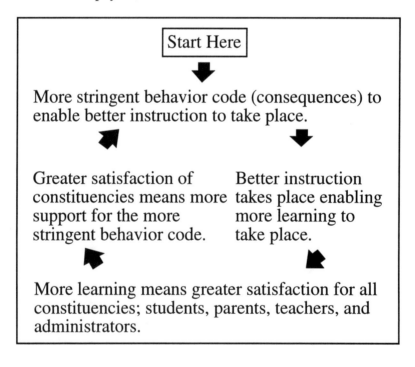

Start Here

More stringent behavior code (consequences) to enable better instruction to take place.

Greater satisfaction of constituencies means more support for the more stringent behavior code.

Better instruction takes place enabling more learning to take place.

More learning means greater satisfaction for all constituencies; students, parents, teachers, and administrators.

Students, in particular, will rebel against a more stringent behavior code that does not provide any new benefits. It's like enacting a new tax to pay off the national debt. Compare this with a community that decides to tax itself to build a new park. This community can experience what its money is going for.

So it is in schools. If students perceive that the only purpose of the discipline changes is to make the teachers or the principal's life easier, they'll say forget it. (Initially, of course, they'll say forget it anyway. They won't believe even when the benefits are introduced. They'll view it is another empty promise.)

But when, through your actions, you demonstrate the payoff, they'll at first merely tolerate, but later come to support the new policies.

Let me give you an example. The first high school in which we instituted ProActive Discipline twelve years ago, had been suffering from (among other ailments) declining enrollment. In its first year of operation under the new system, its population jumped 400 students. After three years, it had a waiting list of almost 500 students seeking admission.

But it was not only the behavior code and discipline policies that had changed. These changes alone would certainly not attract students. The instructional program changed dramatically. It reflected a renewed sense of purpose and concern for each individual student.

One day a student, straight off the street, entered my (the principal's) office. He had dropped out, he said, "pretty much after the fifth grade." He had come to see me because he wanted to enroll.

"Why in the world do you want to come here," I asked. "Our behavior code is more stringent, our standards higher. Surely you'd have an easier time at another more typical high school."

"You don't understand," he said. "The word out on the street is that this place works. If you come here, no matter how far behind you are, this place will take care of you. These teachers care...everybody here cares about you...they'll get you where you need to go no matter how much you've missed...I've done drugs and everything else out there, but I always dreamed there was something better...if you can get me there like the street says you can, then I can handle your rules or anything else..."

In my eyes, this is the greatest compliment this school ever received. And he was right. That staff, those teachers had changed the instructional program. Freed from the bondage of behavior problems, they had created an environment in which it was expected that all kids would succeed. They spent their new-found time, energy (and even money!) on devising ways to pick kids up from where they were and get them where they needed to be. That was their task; that was their job...that was teaching.

And while other schools were experiencing a dropout problem, this school, with its more stringent behavior code and more demanding standards, was experiencing a "drop-in" problem...more students than it could handle.

One final word about payoffs or benefits. Convincing a staff that it can and must provide more benefits to students when the behavior burden is relieved, is not an easy task. In education, we have been conditioned to (as well as comfortable with) the built-in excuses that mitigate our ability and responsibility to bring about universal student learning. Citing lack of attendance, for example, as a barrier to student learning, teachers can easily deflect their responsibility in the learning process. But what if students do show up and what if they are well-behaved, and what if their is administrative support...will teachers be willing to remove themselves from the "convenience of excuses" and shoulder the responsibility for student learning?

Many teachers, you will find, adapt quickly to the new challenge and find new instructional modes and opportunities to help students to achieve as they never had imagined possible.

Some, however, invent new excuses...language, basic skills, etc...until it becomes evident that the only children they are prepared to take responsibility for are those who come to them well-behaved, at grade level, and already knowing what is to be learned. Still others will have difficulty changing from the traditional instructional mode—the teacher-centered lecture—which may have been the only viable means of teaching in prior circumstances but which now, if used exclusively, is ineffective and inefficient.

Nonetheless, substantial effort must be expended through the leadership of the administrators (who now have 80% of their time to devote to supporting instruction) to create the payoff in the classroom for schools if the system is to work. Freed from the demoralizing and time-consuming task of disciplining kids, teachers can now concentrate on figuring out how to help students learn. They can create individual learning plans for each child. They can monitor progress daily, and carefully select learning experiences, based on data, appropriate for each child. This is teaching as it should be...as it can be: taking students where they are, and getting them where they need to be.

SUMMARY: BACK TO LINCOLN HIGH

David Niceguy had no system, no understandable, purpose-driven set of procedures and guidelines within which to operate. The purpose of discipline wasn't clear; the relationship of discipline to everything else that went on in the school had not been established.

"Rights" did not flow automatically to the individual as a result of meeting the prescribed obligations or responsibilities; consequences were neither clearly delineated nor carefully calculated to achieve an overriding educational purpose.

Discipline was there because it always had been; and besides, everybody believed you always needed more of it. And the rules had been the rules since anyone could remember, though sometimes someone would shout loud enough and a committee would be formed who would vehemently reiterate the need for more discipline, shine up the old rules, and pass out revised copies to all faculty members....But...even if Mr. Niceguy had not been saddled with an antiquated system that did not work, even if ProActive Discipline had been in place, he would not have been home-free. For Mr. Niceguy still needed to master the intricacies of implementing the system—making it work.

David Niceguy fulfilled only one-half of the criteria to effectively implement ProActive Discipline. And that one-half, by itself, was enough to get him into a great deal of trouble. Mr. Niceguy possessed a most admirable trait: he was compassionate, he cared about people. He was genuinely concerned about what happened to students. But this trait, ironically, proved his downfall, or at least hastened his downfall as it has many other well-intentioned school administrators. He was but one of a multitude who have unwittingly walked down this path, only to suddenly find themselves vilified by all constituencies and powerless to reverse that image or undo the damage.

David Niceguy did not exhibit the other prime attribute necessary for the successful implementation of ProActive Discipline:

DISCIPLINE MUST BE ADMINISTERED
DISPASSIONATELY BY COMPASSIONATE PEOPLE.

Initially it sounds harsh. It appears to run in the face of much of what we have learned about dealing with young people. Yet, after you have lived with it for a while, you will realize that the most compassionate treatment of children evolves from administering the rules dispassionately.

If we step back in history and view the evolution of the governance of man, we find steady progress toward separation of the law from the individuals charged with enforcing the law. From the time of the Magna Carta, civilization has sought to constrain the monarch to work within the written law rather than outside of it. Our constitution is a guarantee that we as a people will not be subject to the whims and favoritism of the person in power.

We are not content that today's benevolent dictator grants free speech; we are concerned that tomorrow's tyrant may not. We demand that presidents, no matter how well-meaning, work within the constraints of the Constitution.

In short, we want governance through laws rather than men or women. We want to know what is expected of us regardless of who is in power. We want to know what our rights are and we want to know what will happen to those who transgress the laws.

In schools, however, albeit through our genuine concern for children, we have established governance systems in which decisions are based on the individual, rather than the laws. We have reverted to a medieval form of enforcement where the application of the rules and consequences is at the arbitrary discretion of the person applying them.

Kids will share with one another which counselor or assistant principal "will give you the best deal." Like any of us, they will play upon the weakness of the system when they are individually pitted against it, and deride its shortcomings when they view it from a distance.

Most of them can't recite the consequences for a given act as prescribed in the behavior code; but they can tell you what Mr. Smith, or Ms. Jones...or Mr. Niceguy will give you. And they'll describe the circumstances best to invoke when pleading your case: tears, depression, shouts, threats—whatever will work best.

The only real way around this is to apply the rules dispassionately:

When the child does "X"..."Y" will happen."

"X" is the infraction and "Y" is the prescribed consequence. Period.

Once the dispassionate application of the rules has been established, two great benefits follow:

1. The child comes to realize that when he does "X" he is really making "Y" happen. The relationship between choice and consequence is established.

2. The individual administering the consequence is no longer viewed as the "cause" of the consequence. That is, when the entire school community understands (both through the establishment of the rules and automatic consequences; *and* the reinforcement of the relationship between rules and consequences through consistent application) that when John does "X," "Y" will happen, the administration is removed from the contingency loop. The discussion no longer revolves around what Mr. Niceguy will do, rather it centers on what John did. For once it is established that John did "X" everyone understands that "Y" will happen.

Imagine the new position Mr. Niceguy finds himself in. He is no longer the villain. Nor does he shoulder the burden for the entire discipline system. In fact, others can now be involved in the administration of discipline. The procedures are simple, straightforward, understandable—and, dispassionate. The student does "X," "Y" will happen; the student does "A," "B" will happen. No anger, no shouting, no arguments, just the rules.[1]

And, now we have the appropriate opportunity to apply Mr. Niceguy's previously misplaced *compassion.*

---

[1] Space does not permit detailing the nuances of handling the day-to-day "nuts and bolts" routines of ProActive Discipline. Those interested in fuller treatment of the "implementation phase" can consult *The ProActive Discipline Workbook: The Educator's Guide to creating an optimum learning environment,* available through Copernicus Publications, 1760 Creekside Oaks Drive, Suite 290, Sacramento, CA 95833.

For once Mr. Niceguy has explained to the student what the student already knows—that by behaving in this manner (X), he has automatically triggered these consequences (Y)—Mr. Niceguy can begin to help the student pick up the pieces. How do we explain this to Mom or Dad, how do we make sure this doesn't happen again, how do we get back on the right track? Mr. Niceguy's role has changed from adversary to helper. The hour-long session with the student has been transformed into a counseling opportunity. The focus of the meeting is not on whether the consequences will be invoked, but rather on how to deal with the consequences and get the student's life back in order.

Finally, a word of caution is in order here. Do not expect miracles overnight. In creating something new, you must supplant the old. The school must counter time-worn expectations. Picasso said that every act of creation must begin with destruction—destruction of what has been. It will take 3-6 months to establish ProActive Discipline. But once it is up and running, you will never look back!

The difference between a successful person and others is not a lack
of strength, not a lack of knowledge, but rather a lack of will.

                                                    Vince Lombardi

OBSERVATION:

The Only Game In Town

Our children grow up in a world of quick fixes. Take this
for a headache, take this if your back hurts, drink this to feel
happy, and pop this pill to forget your cares. Suddenly they
come to a situation—adolescence—where they are faced with
some of the most complex, mystifying problems of their lives.
As their bodies begin to change, as the peer group tightens its
pressure, our children look in all directions for help. Naturally,
the first places they gravitate to are those which appear to
provide a quick fix. During this period of development, the
school has a tremendous opportunity. If the school understands
and recognizes both the forces it is up against and the power it
possesses, the school can provide the one safe opportunity for
children to experience a good time without having to resort to
the quick fixes.

Here's how it works. Let me describe what we call the "only
game in town" leverage factor.

The school is the only place where, as a young person, you
can go and meet large numbers of your peers on an everyday
basis. It is also the only place in town where social activities are
organized on an ongoing basis. In other words, much of the
strong motivation for attending school centers around the
opportunity to mix with peers, particularly those of the opposite
sex. (And we thought they just wanted to come to learn!)

Now, the school can either assume that its only obligation is
in the area of books, pencils, tests, and term papers; or it can
grasp the reality of this situation and capitalize on it.

If the school uses the "only game in town" concept to leverage its position, it will find that it has a "once-in-a-lifetime" opportunity to help each child. First and most obvious, the school can induce students to attend and further their academic achievement by holding out the carrot of co-curricular activities. But, just as important, the school can use this opportunity to provide perhaps the one chance in a lifetime for the student to experience happiness, joy, fulfillment, and fun without resorting to quick fixes—the uppers and downers, the drugs, the alcohol—to pave the way. During this short span of time, four years of high school, two in middle school, the school has the opportunity to instill within children the concept that they can, indeed, have a good time while remaining straight...and "clean."

In order to do this, however, the school must not only understand the leverage that it possesses, it must also understand the dynamics of what's going on and be willing to make use of its leverage. In short, the school must take advantage of the fact that it is the "only game in town."

It must tell students that to get a ticket to the "only game in town," they must meet certain requirements. One of these requirements is maintaining good grades and another is being absolutely straight at activities. In some community cultures, this means no drugs before you arrive and nothing behind the back parking lot or in the restrooms. In other cultures, it means no beer down by the levee before you hit the dance.

Regardless of what a particular neighborhood dictates, it is critical that the school take this hard-line posture. This can prove difficult especially when the school across town or in another city remains oblivious to the fact that it has this same "only game in town" opportunity. Even parents will rebel; they will say "What difference does one glass of champagne make before graduation or a couple of beers before the homecoming dance?" Some will even be tolerant of drugs used "in moderation" prior to attending these school functions. And they will make excuses for their kids. They will tell you that these are the 1990's and that the school has no right to have these expectations.

I would contend that it is more than a right, it is a responsibility; but beyond a right or a responsibility, it is a tremendous opportunity! If the school and the school community will come together, unite, take the hard-line, and hold kids accountable (and, yes, even initially keep some students away from activities), they will find that their activities will be better attended and more upbeat.

Schools all over the country who have taken this hard-line approach attest to this phenomenon. I can tell you that I've observed it and that it really works.[1] I can also tell you that, once again, it is not easy. You must be willing to fight some battles; but if you truly believe, after you've looked around, that school is the "only game in town," then it behooves you to make use of that opportunity in the best interest of the children who attend.

It took us almost six months to begin to reap the benefits when we first put this concept into place.

We took the hard-line. We said, "A little bit (drugs or alcohol) is not O.K." The answer is either yes or no. This is a binary problem. Either yes you're clean, or no you're not. If you're clean, you can get in and participate, if you're not, you can't. Period.

"...What's more, if you're not clean, you probably can't go to school here anymore. And this is a good place to be. You just got yourself thrown out of the 'only game in town.'"

---

[1] Again you must "ensure the benefits." In "Football, chearleaders and other stuff that matters," we described the creation of a football program that vast numbers of students wanted to experience. As a result, we had no problem requiring a "C+" average for participation.

We told kids we would have the greatest activities in the world, and we would support whatever they wanted in every way possible, but these activities would be clean. Period.

It worked. We had the only game in town. And, one night, as I looked around the crowded dance floor and saw all of these kids having a great time, I thought maybe, at some later time, they could look back to at least one period in their lives when, unaided by quick fixes, they were really having fun. Maybe they would remember that "the only game in town" was worth the price of admission.

STEP 3 CHECKLIST

- ❏ Develop the rationale for discipline
- ❏ Determine the underlying principles
- ❏ Establish the social contract
- ❏ Understand the 80/20 time trap
- ❏ Streamline policies and procedures
- ❏ Ensure consistent application of rules

STEP 4

DEVELOP ORGANIZATIONAL READINESS

- *OBSERVATION: A Pox on Those Little Smiling Faces (or A Look at the Other Side of Self-Esteem)*

- *DEVELOP ORGANIZATIONAL READINESS*

- *STEP 4 CHECKLIST*

My best friend is the one who brings out the best in me.

Henry Ford

OBSERVATION:

A Pox On Those Little Smiling Faces
(Or A Look At The Other Side Of Self-Esteem)

It has always seemed odd to me that in so many human ventures when we set out to accomplish one thing, we unwittingly seem to accomplish exactly the opposite. When we're in the water struggling to stay afloat, we sink; and when we don't worry about sinking, we float. When we go on diets, we end up gaining weight; when we try to relax, we get uptight. We spend our leisure time getting exhausted.

What happens, in simplistic terms, is that we seldom completely define the problem. The partially-defined or ill-defined problem suggests a quick and immediate fix. And that fix is oftentimes counterproductive.

So it is with the concern in recent years about "self-esteem." We have correctly predicted what low self-esteem will cause, i.e., lack of confidence, fear to act, failure to believe in one's own capabilities. Sincerely concerned about these outcomes, we have quickly defined the problem as "lack of self-esteem" and put in place numerous programs and concepts geared to quickly and effortlessly restore self-esteem in children.

Unfortunately, much like the swimmer struggling to survive, many of these programs and the attitudes that they have fostered among school staffs and parents have had the opposite effect.

Here's how it works. The child produces work; the teacher looks at the work and recognizes it for what it is: work that is less than acceptable. In the old days she would have put a "D" grade on top of the paper and handed it back. Now, having been thoroughly trained in how to build self-esteem in young people, she stamps a happy face on top, and gently scrawls underneath "Good work, Brian. Keep trying."

Now Brian gets the paper back and takes a look and determines one of two things:

1) "I guess this teacher doesn't know much about what's going on if this is the kind of grade she gives."

or

2) "I guess she doesn't really think I can do much better than this."

Let's get one thing straight from the beginning; Brian is no dummy. Whether in kindergarten or a sophomore in high school, Brian knows good work when he sees it. He experiences the work of the children around him and can pretty much determine where his work fits into the continuum. Brian thinks, but is really not sure, that he could do better. His teacher could have reinforced this fact by giving Brian an honest estimate of how well he had done. But instead, in the interest of preserving or promoting Brian's "self-esteem," she has, with all good intentions, deceived him. She has told him something was "good" or "adequate" when it was not.

Now Brian really has something to figure out. He knows that within the classroom there is a much higher quality of work than he has turned in. But the question Brian has to ask (usually somewhat subconsciously) is whether he, in fact, is capable of turning in better work.

The one and only authority figure in the room—the one person who really ought to know—the teacher, has apparently told him that this is about as good as he can do. She has told him that she does not expect more from him. Brian understands this. He knows that his parents did not expect his seven month old baby sister to talk. Parents and adults—and especially teachers—certainly know what to expect from children…

And so Brian, through a sort of inverted logic, finally determines that this is about as good as he can do. The authority figure in the classroom has told him that and continues to reinforce it with smiling faces on the top of his papers. Substandard work is continually accepted from Brian. Brian, in turn, views this as indicative of his ability level.

Ironically, in an effort to nurture Brian's self-esteem, his teacher has, in fact, decreased it. In a patronizing way, the school has said to Brian: "You aren't a very good student, Brian. Just do the best you can." And Brian, like most children, is very good at taking his cues from adults and authority figures.

But what if the school had been more honest with Brian and more demanding of him? What if his teacher, through the papers that are handed back and the continual personal interactions, said to Brian:

"You can do better than this, Brian; I know you have the ability. I know you can produce better work."

Brian is now hearing from the authority figure a statement (ideally reinforced time and again) that he is better than the work he has produced. This authority figure believes in Brian. This authority figure will not allow Brian to work at a level below his potential.

It seems that in our rush to define the problem, we have confused the concept of respect with self-esteem. We have fallen into the overachiever syndrome where who I am is determined by what I produce. When Brian produces less than acceptable work, we cannot really confront Brian with this reality, or it will surely diminish his personhood. In other words, Brian *is* what Brian produces.

But, if we start with a basic concept of human respect whereby all children are respected and worthy of our caring and concern by virtue of the simple fact that they are human beings, regardless of the quality of work they perform...if we can instill in Brian that he is valued— separate and distinct from what he produces—we can then go about the process of accurately assessing his work.

When we begin to separate the concept of basic human respect from that of self-esteem, we can begin to attack the problem that, incidentally, does exist. And, if we genuinely believe that all children can learn, then we must begin to accurately assess the work they produce and give them feedback which will enable them to progress.

The concept is really simple. Think back in your own life. Think to those "gladhanders" who congratulated you when you knew you didn't deserve it. Think of those others. Those mentors, those role models, those teachers, who demanded from you your very best. Their message came through loud and clear:

YOU CAN DO IT!

When children witness the improved quality of their own work, they gain genuine self-esteem; and from this self-esteem emanates the confidence necessary for them to take on larger and more difficult pursuits.

Now I know there are reasons, you will tell me, why this can't happen in the average classroom. Class size, differences in ability level, lack of sufficient time, etc., etc., but there has to be a way... a way for the average teacher to be able to say to each child:

"You, as a human being, are worthy of my respect and you shall have it. And because I believe in you and I believe in your ability and potential as a human being, I will expect from you a quality of work that meets that high standard of performance that you are capable of...

And when you do not meet this level of performance, I will tell you, and I will counsel you, and I will assist you...

Because that is my job as a teacher...

To bring out the very best in you."

In the absence of clearly defined goals, we are forced to concentrate on activity and ultimately become enslaved by it.

Chuck Conradt
The Game of Work

STEP 4: DEVELOP ORGANIZATIONAL READINESS

In establishing a level playing field, the rules of conduct and interaction are delineated. The "purposeful pursuit of educational goals" becomes the standard by which all activity is measured. The human climate necessary to sustain growth and change, as well as teaching and learning are prescribed. A social contract is established.

In Step 4, we ensure that the organizational structure is capable of supporting change. To assume that the structure, as it exists, can quickly adapt is to court disaster. If the organization cannot respond to the new demands of the changing school, the change process will come to a grinding halt. Probably more than any other of the 7 Steps or preconditions, this is the most overlooked.

Yet it stands to reason, if you're going to change how people think and act, you had better recognize that the old organization will have difficulty supporting these new behaviors. There are three prime areas that must be addressed: administrative structure, decision analysis capabilities, and data access.

1. *Administrative Structure*

Take a look at how the school is currently organized. Does it make sense for a dynamic and responsive learning organization to be structured like this? Probably not. Check the functions, new and old, that administrators are expected to carry out. Prioritize them. Redefine jobs, classifications, responsibilities. Work with an administrative staff to develop a model that you are convinced is the best equipped to carry out your change agenda—and administer the new school.

This task can be effectively addressed by creating what we call a Mission Diagram. This diagram emanates from the newly re-defined "mission" or "purpose" of the school. It extends the mission to include the various functions which must be carried out. It further lists who is responsible for each function. As a "wall chart" permanently displayed in a conspicuous place, the Mission Diagram is an invaluable tool in restructuring.

Then move to the teaching staff. Are there better ways to organize for the delivery of instruction? At this point you will probably find few answers because the school's strategic action plan has not yet been fully developed. No one is really sure exactly what changes will be proposed. But it is important, nonetheless, to begin to ask the questions...to begin to explore new and different staff organizational concepts that can better serve the needs of students. For, once these questions or possibilities are raised, staff can file them for future reference as they explore various instructional and operational options to achieve their mission.

2. Decision Analysis Capabilities

Who will be involved in decisions? How will decisions be made? What data must be available to make optimum decisions? These questions, again, must be asked prior to confronting new issues. The structure for decision analysis which evolves must enable leadership to react quickly and correctly to numerous new situations.

We are told that the average principal makes about 500 decisions per week. That's 100 per day, or roughly 12 per hour. Some of these decisions are simple and require very little research or investigation of facts; others are complex and require (or should require) the collection of extensive data as well as the evaluation of alternatives.

Research indicates that school leaders make decisions in a variety of contexts with varying degrees of skill. We are concerned about the quality of the decisions that are made in schools because ultimately what springs from the quality of the decisions is the quality of the school.

Technology is available to assist in decision analysis as well. A multiple–criteria decision analysis framework developed by a group of professors out of Kansas State University[1] has recently been adapted for use in schools. (This is the same technology we utilize in weighting the Successful Student Assessment Model (S[2]AM) criteria.)

This type of technology can provide schools and districts with assistance in a variety of critical decision areas including budget formulation, staff selection, and resource allocation. But regardless of the method you employ, Decision Analysis is critical to school change. You must develop a system and pre-plan how major decisions will be made, who will be involved, and who must be consulted. Decisions cannot be approached in a haphazard manner. You must be prepared and equipped to make even more decisions of even greater magnitude as you initiate change in a school.

3. *Data Access*

If you've made an airline reservation lately or have simply stopped by your bank, you will know that these institutions could not have survived if they had continued to operate as they did twenty, ten, or even five years ago. Schools, too, must take advantage of the office automation systems that are out there. But until schools, like airlines and banks,[2] become outcome driven, (that is judged by their success in educating students) they will continue to assert that they cannot afford automation.

As soon as schools become outcome or client-driven or as soon as they begin competing for students with the advent of

---

[1] Now functioning as HTX International, Inc., Manhattan, Kansas.

[2] Do you realize that before 1983, there were no automated teller systems? Now, they are an integral part of most people's daily financial activities.

"choice," they will realize that they cannot afford not to automate their practices. Such thinking is on the horizon.

Welcome to the 21st century!

The school with as many as 2,000 students and 150 teachers needs to provide administrators with the capability to react quickly and decisively based upon good information. The only way to do this is to automate the collection, processing and analysis of data.

While a number of systems have been developed, one of the most innovative and creative comes from a small company called Slipstream Solutions.[1] Its creativity and adaptability stems, in no small part, from the fact that its founders were themselves middle school teachers. As such, they faced, daily, the frustrating inability to access student records, generate continuous communication with parents, etc.

Other equally affordable systems are available. Some school districts have created their own. But, regardless of how you do it, it is essential to realize that the old structure—the old way of doing things—simply won't be able to support the new dynamic school. Begin the process of organizational redesign and retooling early. Anticipate your needs. Once you are in the throes of change, it will be difficult to stop and create new systems.

---

[1] Slipstream Solutions, Inc., Denver, Colorado.

STEP 4 CHECKLIST

- ❏ Adjust administrative/organizational structure
- ❏ Construct an effective decision analysis framework
- ❏ Facilitate data collection/handling/access

These unhappy times call for the building of plans…that build from the bottom up and not from the top down…

Franklin D. Roosevelt

STEP 5

CREATE A BLUEPRINT FOR CHANGE

- *OBSERVATION: A Question of Size*

- *CREATE A BLUEPRINT FOR CHANGE*

- *STEP 5 CHECKLIST*

When you have got an elephant by the hind legs and he is trying to run away, it's best to let him go.

                                        Abraham Lincoln

OBSERVATION:

A Question Of Size

American schools were designed to reflect the bigger-is-better theory of organizations. Cost savings are immediately realized when two schools of one thousand students are combined into one school of two thousand students. Dual management structures, dual cafeterias, dual maintenance areas, dual bus schedules are eliminated as schools increase in size. When we look at schools from an input-based model (the input being the number of children who can be serviced for the fewest dollars) this seems to make sense.

When we begin to look at schools from an output vantage point, the picture changes. Efficiencies realized in larger schools belie the effectiveness of the organization in achieving its purpose. When the school of two thousand has a dropout rate of 40% while schools of one thousand have a dropout rate of 15%, certainly the outcome for students is affected by size.

Most of our schools are just too big to nurture learning. Many have become cold, uncaring institutions which have no time to meet needs of individual students.

The simplest and quickest way to facilitate learning in America is to make schools smaller. This one act would probably do more to improve the school experience for young people than any other single move we could make.

Studies indicate that certain school size foster learning. Roughly speaking, when a high school exceeds 1,800 students, a middle school 600 and an elementary school 500, we begin to lose the personal touch so important to learning.

Significantly smaller schools suffer from an inability to afford broad programs. Staff can't offer the background and expertise to support a the full range of curriculum.

While the numbers may vary, the fact remains that downsizing is the simplest, most profound means of countering the dehumanizing climate in our schools. This often requires difficult political maneuvering in changing student populations from one location to another![1]

Yet, there are two (and probably many) alternatives to the actual physical process of making schools smaller. While not achieving the full benefits of the small school, these alternatives make significant strides toward humanizing schools.

The first is the school-within-a-school concept.[2] In this configuration, students—along with teachers, administrators, and support personnel—are divided into subgroups. These subgroups provide the young person with a sense of identity and belonging.

Developing the school-within-a-school concept is not all that difficult. It requires a willingness on the part of administration to divide its responsibilities. It requires that staff design and adapt a new curriculum. In some cases, it can require physical alteration of facilities.

The school-within-a-school concept will work when those initiating it understand and embrace its purpose—to provide a closer substructure for students. Variations on the theme of schools-within-a-school are numerous. At one extreme, each school entity is entirely independent, creating its own curriculum, set of rules, regulations, and expectations. At the other extreme, the school-within-a-school functions under the over-arching umbrella of the larger school whose policies and procedures continue to direct the separate school segments.

---

[1] Have you ever tried to change school attendance boundaries in a district? A nightmare!

[2] Variations on this theme include the "cluster," "core," or "pod" configurations.

A second alternative makes each adult within the school responsible for a small number of students (10 to 20). The elementary school, of course, requires that a teacher account for all aspects of the child's school life: academic progress, behavior, attendance, and special help. Secondary schools assign counselors to this function, but typically, a high school counselor is responsible for 300-500 students.

When we first tried breaking down these numbers, we took the student body of two thousand and divided it in half alphabetically: A through L, M through Z. We took our two assistant principals and put one in charge of each group. We did the same with our two deans. We split our four counselors: two for each group.

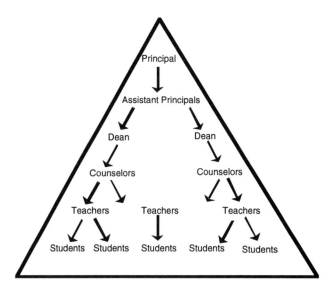

We then took the entire certificated staff—including teachers, nurses, and librarians—and divided that group by two. We proceeded then to divide each half of the student body by the number of certificated staff to supervise them. The end result: every certificated staff member (most of whom were teachers) was assigned about fourteen students.

All adults bore responsibility for the success of their assigned students. They would meet formally in a classroom setting once each week (called guidance class) and also with the individual students at different times throughout the week. During these sessions, they would talk to the kids about grades, attendance, behavior, graduation requirements, college admissions, and any other subjects that needed to be covered.

Initially, some staff members became concerned. They did not know graduation or college admission requirements. A physics teacher was working with a student who wanted to be a contractor; a woodshop instructor was working with a budding biologist. Counselors took on the obligation of providing staff with the training, materials, and guidance needed to work with these students. If a staff member could not answer a question, he or she simply said, "I'll have that for you in twenty-four hours," and then proceeded to the counselor for help.

Some students in a guidance group were ninth graders, some tenth, some eleventh, and some twelfth. Some were worrying about graduation and college or work; others were worrying about how to make it through tenth grade biology. The interplay among ages proved extremely beneficial. Seniors were giving ninth graders advice which they wished someone had given them. Juniors were talking to sophomores about what classes to take next year.

The staff member maintained assignments of students throughout the four years of the student's high school career. Each year, the seniors in his or her group would graduate and ninth graders would replace them. Staff worked very closely with students on an individual basis. Some found this difficult; most found it rewarding.

Every student was issued a guidance folder for recording grades, co-curricular activities, goals for college, and/or future work possibilities.

At the end of each semester, grades were distributed by the guidance teacher. Each student would take this computer printout and transcribe grades by hand into the guidance folder. Carefully, the student would check off any required courses completed and write in the number of units achieved.

I cannot describe the "magic" in this simple task. Certainly it has something to do with the kinesthetic or tactile activity of manually recording one's own grades and progress. Just as important, however, it serves as a psychological pat-on-the-back each time the student can account for a classroom accomplishment. Accomplishments in athletics, music, the arts, and other areas were duly recorded in the folder. At the end of a student's senior year, the fruits and the labor of the four-year high school experience were reflected.

Making schools smaller is not really the answer; the answer is to make schools more responsive to individual students. When we do make schools smaller, however, we move toward achieving this end. But if making schools smaller is an impossibility, look to other avenues to achieve this end.

In education, the structure works against us. We must maintain vigilance to ensure that it does not force us into behaviors that are counter-productive. We want all children to be successful. Major components in accomplishing this are individual attention, consideration, and concern. Yet, in our quest for efficiency, we have made our schools big and cold. We must seek ways to break down the "bigness" and "coldness" and work with the individual child.

The key is to understand how vital this personal caring is to the educational success of young people. Personal caring can even overshadow, or make livable, a school's other deficiencies.

Caring breeds tolerance. Both ways.

The harder you push, the harder the system pushes back.

Peter Senge
The Fifth Discipline

STEP 5: CREATE A BLUEPRINT FOR CHANGE

Strategic planning sounds so simple—create a plan and put that plan into action. Nothing to it. Find a good idea for your school and get staff and community to embrace it. Carefully write out who will do what, when, how, where—and then implement.

The only problem is that if you're an educator, you've been through this more times than you'd like to admit. Because schools have been resistant to change, and because they have been the subject of much public concern, a new concept or idea seems to come to full bloom every other minute. Each fall as teachers arrive to begin their assignments, they are typically greeted with a new panacea that will solve all problems, save all children, and make the community quite happy with its school. (See the Holy Grail Observation.)

The principal is sure this is the answer. Enthusiastically, he or she goes about recruiting staff and community to support the new concept. This gives rise to the formation of committees. Schools can't function without committees. And these committees, through the diligent toil of the members, create written documents, carefully copied and distributed to all staff. These documents usually find their way to a binder, and the binder to a shelf. This is about as far as it goes and everyone relaxes until the next "answer" comes along.

The first few times through this, staff members are excited. But after having seen this scenario played out time and again, teachers, as well as community leaders, become cynical. They have witnessed the great enthusiasm at the initiation of the project, the ensuing ground swell of support, only to look back a year later and observe that the program hadn't really made any difference.

As we have said, if real school change were easy, it would already have occurred. School change requires disengaging from a mode of operation that has been in existence for almost 100 years. (Imagine our world if engineering, medical science, or industrial technology had changed as little from the turn of the century as education!)

The problem lies in the complex interactions and underpinnings of the school's organizational structure. We say that...

"the seeds of the destruction of any good idea—and most of the ideas for school reform are good ideas—currently exist within the school itself."

In other words, the likelihood or probability of failure in attempting to change the school is very high because of the level of resistance within the existing school structure.

Regardless of the endeavor—whether in government, schools, or personal weight-loss—the pursuit of change begins like this: once we consciously determine that we are not getting, the results we want, we decide it's time for change. ("If you always do what you've always done, you'll always get what you always got.")[1]

After experiencing this dissatisfaction with the status quo, those who seek change follow this basic pattern:

Mission › Plan › Action = Results

The terms may change, but the concepts are the same. The mission or desired outcome drives the plan which, in turn,

---

[1] This, incidentally, is why schools have real trouble motivating change: their assessment methods do not create a sufficient level of dissatisfaction to inspire change. Test scores, that only PhDs can decipher, or absences rates, that sound low because they allow so many exceptions, do not provide real incentives to change the way schools operate. As a result, most pressure for school change emanates from outside rather than inside the system. But this, as you recall, moves us into a whole different area. (See Step 2—Create a Method of Scorekeeping.)

drives the action or changed behavior. When all goes well, this changed behavior brings about new or changed results. These results are tangible indicators, the assessment, that the mission is being accomplished.

Unless the projected results are clearly spelled out and correspond directly to the mission, change will not occur because...it is the projected results that motivate the changes in behavior; or as we have said before:

Assessment Drives Change

But let's suppose, again in the generic enterprise,[1] that we have developed a mission, generated a strategic action plan, and depicted tangible and meaningful results that serve as motivators to action. Can we predict success?

The answer is still, "No." The fact is that most plans fail. And they fail because they neglect one key piece of the puzzle: the existing environment. No plan is put into action in a vacuum; no plan unfolds in isolation. There is an environment, a culture, a history, a tradition—standard procedures, a set way of doing things—upon which the plan must intrude.

Therefore, our little diagram leaves out a key element in the change process. The diagram should look like this:

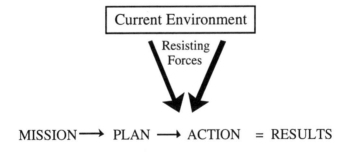

MISSION ⟶ PLAN ⟶ ACTION = RESULTS

---

[1] Again, this model is generic, so we're talking about any human endeavor—from launching missiles to physical fitness!

The arrows depicting the resisting forces impact the sequence primarily at the point of action. Until that time, they lay dormant within the organization. They surface only when the status quo is threatened, and the better the plan, or the more radical departure from the status quo, the greater the resistance.

This resistance is projected through individuals and takes the form of:

❏ Inertia	Protection of the status quo
❏ Bureaucracy	Rules, procedures, red tape
❏ Self-Preservation	"...but I've taught the same class for 15 years."
❏ Organizational Structure	"What you propose simply cannot fit within our framework."
❏ Established Culture	"We don't do things like that."
❏ Miscellaneous	"We'll find some reason why we can't do it."

Physics tells us that inertia can only be counteracted by an equal and opposite force. The problem is that seldom does the "force for change" equal the resisting force the organization can muster even at a moment's notice. Couple this with the fact that these resisting forces are deceptive in nature—that is, they throw us off guard by echoing all of the rhetoric of change while concealing their destructive intent—and the problem is magnified.

That is why most plans for change end up like this:

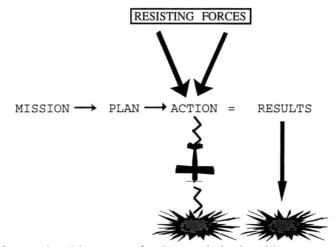

If we take this a step further and depict this on a vertical scale, moving the "results" down to the same level as the defused action, we also realize that this effort failed to accomplish anything of significance—status-quo triumphed again!

This is why schools often accomplish a watered-down version or a trace of what they had intended. The resisting forces allow action only at a level that is not threatening to the organization.

But the worst aspect of this whole sequence is that this resistence is not the result of calculated deceit and intrigue among staff. No, instead it arises from this mindless beast called the "organization" or in this case, the "school." This effective scuttling of change is actually the product of complex interactions of well-meaning individuals doing what they think is right for the profession, for the school—and for the children! The school can't even surface a villain—which further disempowers it.

Take away the cause and the effect ceases.

Miguel de Cervantes

In the early 1970's, Dr. Kent Stephens, a university professor, realized the tremendous resistance to change generated by organizations even though those within the organization appeared to be very receptive to new ideas. Dr. Stephen's research in Failure Avoidance Technology resulted in his development of the *Sage Analysis*.[1]

In simple terms, the *Sage Analysis* predicts and graphically depicts where and how a plan or new idea will fail. In a school, this means that as you set in motion a plan to bring about substantive change, you also predict where the plan will meet resistance and what will cause it to fail to live up to its expectations.

Predicting resistance—where, when, and how it will surface—and confronting it head-on, before it defuses the strategic action plan, is critical to creating and sustaining school change. First, you must identify it and trace it through cause-effect logic to its source. Then you can develop counteractive strategies and integrate them into your strategic plan.

In short, you must not only create a strategic action plan, you must "failsafe" its implementation.

The strategic plan is like a hybrid seed carefully developed in the laboratory and sure to be successful if it is planted in soil that is receptive, soil that will provide it with the nutrients to grow and prosper. Unfortunately, in education, our tendency is to drop the fertile seed (the exciting new idea) onto uncultivated ground. We take the carefully developed plan to implement this exciting new idea and superimpose it on an organization and an organizational structure that will snuff out its life. Therefore, before taking a plan to the launching pad, it is essential to...

Fail the plan on paper.

---

[1] *Sage Analysis* is proprietary to Sage Analytics, International, Inc., Provo, Utah.

Practice failure avoidance, either formally through technology such as Sage Analysis, or informally through group brainstorming processes and open solicitation of failure modes. You'll be surprised at the responses. Make sure to seek input from staff who may not normally participate. You need multiple perspectives. (Sage Analysis utilizes a detailed survey of all staff.)

Simply ask: "Based upon your experience in this school, why will this plan fail?"

Or "How will it fail?"

Then compile your data and integrate into your strategic action plan steps to neutralize or eliminate these resisting forces.

Undoubtedly you will be accosted at some juncture for being so negative. "Why are we spending all this time talking about failure?" The answer from Dr. Stephens himself is:

"What is more positive than avoiding failure and how can you avoid it if you don't understand it; and how can you understand it if you don't analyze for it?"

Remember, once you have a mission in place and clearly defined outcomes (results), building a plan is relatively easy. Bring together an appropriate group and delineate what needs to be done, who is responsible, timelines, benchmarks, etc.

The hard part is taking action (Step 6). But you can greatly facilitate the Action Step if, while creating the plan you anticipate and define the most probable resisting forces. To do this, you must leave the enthusiasm and excitement of change behind for a moment and soberly address the prospect of failure. Again, it is a fact that:

Most Plans Fail!

This is your best opportunity to buy some "success insurance" and move your plan out of the "most" realm.

If you plan correctly, your depiction of the change process should actually look like this:

MISSION ⟶ PLAN ⟶ ACTION   =   RESULTS

Now to the Action!

STEP 5 CHECKLIST

☐ Review the Mission

☐ Assess current "results"

☐ Clearly spell out the new intended results

☐ Create a plan to achieve the results

☐ Face reality: *Most Plans Fail*

☐ Identify the resisting forces within the environment which will oppose the plan (fail the plan on paper)

☐ Incorporate action to neutralize or counteract the resisting forces (failsafe the plan)

We will either find a way or make one.

Hannibal

STEP 6

TAKE ACTION

- *OBSERVATION: Dropouts, Attendance, and the Perry Como Solution*

- *TAKE ACTION*

- *STEP 6 CHECKLIST*

When a man sits with a pretty girl for an hour, it seems like a minute; but let him sit on a hot stove for a minute—and it's longer than an hour. That's relativity.

Albert Einstein

OBSERVATION:

Dropouts, Attendance, And The Perry Como Solution

Traditionally we have viewed the dropout problem as a "student problem." We have, as a result, sought to solve the dropout problem by changing the student. Take a look at the numerous dropout programs funded by the federal government and various other well-meaning foundations. You will find that these programs center around changing the behavior and the attitudes of the students.

Now, while none of this is wrong, it is based upon an incomplete definition of the dropout problem. Let's look at the dropout problem in its simplest terms:

THE STUDENT DOES NOT ATTEND SCHOOL

Notice, however, that there are two nouns, not one, in this statement. The first is the subject of the sentence: student; the other is the object of the sentence: school.

If we once again view the school as a konstant, that is, unchangeable, we are forced to spend all of our time and energy changing the behavior of students so that they can fit into the mold of the school.

Have we ever considered that maybe the school needs changing; maybe schools cause dropouts?

Reflect for a moment; suppose I were to give you two envelopes, each containing fifty concert tickets, and ask you to proceed to any high school or middle school cafeteria and distribute these tickets free of charge to young people. Now, in the envelope in your left pocket are the tickets to a Perry Como concert. In your right pocket are tickets to an MC Hammer, Bruce Springstein, or even Grateful Dead concert.

Which pocket would be empty first?

I am not suggesting that we make our schools into rap or rock auditoriums. I am simply stating that in this situation, the students remain konstant, but the activity varies. And, when the activity varies, we find the students ready and excited to attend. The same students who turn down tickets to the Perry Como concert, anxiously wait in long lines in hope of receiving tickets to the MC Hammer concert.

I submit, then, that the students who day in and day out "turn down" our schools and become the attendance problems and the dropouts, are the same students who will readily attend when their schools offer something that is meaningful to them.

Let me summarize thus far. In accepting the fact that there is both a subject and an object in the sentence which describes the dropout problem, ie. THE STUDENT DOES NOT ATTEND SCHOOL, we have recognized that there is another battlefront in education. This, of course, once again is based upon the assumption that the school can change, that it truly is a variable and not simply a konstant. In our desire to solve the dropout problem, we have jumped to the conclusion that the school is "OK," and that the problem lies inherently in the student.[1] "If we could only change the kids, make them like they used to be 20 or 30 years ago, everything would be all right."

Well, not only is this an impossibility, but it also runs contrary to logic. We live in a fast-paced, action-packed world, spinning at twice the speed of twenty and thirty years ago, yet we expect students whose lives are now filled with constant activity and continual stimuli to suddenly leave that world and passively occupy a seat for six hours a day.

---

[1] Or we may have decided that changing the school is a hopeless endeavor, so we might as well concentrate on the student. Regardless, the outcome is the same.

As a principal, I had a standing invitation for any staff member to spend a day living the life of a student. Randomly, we would select a student's locator card. (This card lists the sequence of classes the student takes each period of the day.) The teacher's day, then, would be spent doing exactly what that student would do—walking from class to class. At the end of the day, teachers would tell me that they were absolutely exhausted. As if being in a sitting position for six hours a day were not enough, these teachers also complained that they found themselves being in a passive rather than active position for six constant hours. There was no opportunity for them to creatively use their energies. For much of the day, they were required to sit and listen. Occasionally, their task was to individually and quietly complete an assignment. On rare occasions, they worked with other students and were allowed to make some noise. This is the Perry Como[1] concert that we send our kids to; the tune we expect them to dance to in the 90's. Is it any wonder they pass up our free tickets?

Frankly, I am amazed at the large numbers of students who do *not* dropout. As parents and as educators, we are to be congratulated in that we have been able to coerce, manipulate, and discipline our children enough to have them attend this outdated concert on a day-to-day basis.

But I often wonder whether our dropouts aren't in reality our smartest kids; whether, in fact, they are the ones with the sufficient initiative and self-confidence to buck the system and say "I won't take this anymore."

We are speaking here, of course, in very general terms. There are dynamic and exciting teachers out there whose enthusiasm and day-to-day caring encourages large numbers of students to attend school. But, we are also simply stating the obvious—that students dropout for a reason, (at a rate of 3,000

---

[1] I personally have nothing against Perry Como. I like much of his music. Obviously he is used by way of general example. Please excuse me, Perry.

per day!) that reason being that the system as it currently exists, has become more and more difficult to tolerate and continues to fall behind the pace of the outside world.

In our informal research, with large numbers of students who do attend school, we find that their reasons typically center around one or two classes, teachers, or supportive individuals who keep them coming to school. For some, it is making it through the school day to participate in athletics; for others, it's Ms. Smith's English class, or counselor Jones' encouragement that makes the difference.

In our own real life experience, we walked into a high school with about a 20% absence rate and roughly the same number of dropouts. After completely dismantling the school's structure, we established its student-centered purpose, and then built the structure back piece by logical piece. We found that within the short span of one year, the absence rate had dropped to 3.4% and dropouts were flocking back to the school. The second year of operation, the absence rate dropped to 2.4% and in the third year, 1.8%. The school went from a declining enrollment, losing 150 students a year, to a maximum enrollment (all seats were full) with a waiting list of 500.

But what we also found, which was just as enlightening, was that it didn't take an MC Hammer "payoff" to get kids to come to school. (One of our early detractors claimed that the only way you would get kids to attend would be to teach a curriculum of "sex and motorcycles.") On the contrary, what we did find was that students were hungry for the "scraps" of education that would make a difference in their lives, and were more than willing to give us the benefit of a doubt as we toiled (sometimes less than effectively) to make their education meaningful.

And that was the key—meaningful education—having it mean something to them—making it perfectly plain and clear that it was in their best interest to attend school and setting up the school so that it truly acted out this message.

Children, we found, will attend readily if what happens relates to them, helps them, and is provided in a warm and caring environment.

To our amazement, I guess we found out that kids are no different from the rest of us.

There is a tide in the affairs of men,

Which, taken at the flood, leads on to fortune;

Omitted, all the voyage of their life

Is bound in shallows and miseries.

William Shakespeare

STEP 6: TAKE ACTION

This is it! Lights...Camera...Action! To this point, you have:

> Created a change mindset
> Determined how to keep score
> Created an optimum teaching/learning environment
> Readied the office and organizational structure to accept change
> Put together a realistic blueprint for action...

But none of this makes any difference if you don't successfully complete Step 6. Without successfully taking action, you are simply back to the "old circumvention route" taken by schools for years. Schools, you understand by now, do not readily accept change. But, as organizations, they have evolved an ingenious method of dealing with the pressure to change: they "study" it; they "plan" it; they "committee"[1] it.

LEADERS FORM COMMITMENTS
—FOLLOWERS FORM *COMMITTEES*

The typical lifecycle of an idea terminates by suffocation in committee. To take action, then, means to wage war, openly, against the status quo and that includes committee inaction!

There are five critical elements in taking action; each must be undertaken from a battlefront mentality. Do not be lulled into believing that making change happen in your school won't be a battle. Know that your enemy—this unthinking bureaucracy—is clever and skillful at deflecting new ideas and concepts—just look at its track record!

1. *Orchestrate*: To orchestrate is to provide clear and ongoing instruction—written and verbal—about how to carry out the change.

Your strategic plan and your subsequent tactical plans (the hands-on, "how to" directions) are the basis for developing these "implementation instructions." But you must remember, you will be orchestrating change in a variety of areas simultaneously: behavior, attendance, curriculum, instruction, school-day organization, etc. Prepare a separate room resplendent with wall charts upon which you can track the progress of each change. A war room.

2. *Monitor:* Develop a schedule whereby you and your staff can oversee each new operation on an hourly basis. This is Tom Peter's[2] "Management by Walking Around." We call it

---

[1] "Committee" is used here as a verb, as in "We won't have any more problems with that idea....I committeed it."

[2] Peters and Waterman; *In Search of Excellence*, 1982.

"Nobody in their Office Time," and we expect all personnel not assigned to teaching at that time to assist in monitoring. This is the only way to spot potential problems in time to do something about them.

3. *Receive Feedback:* Of course, all of the monitoring will do no good if there isn't feedback. Do not expect feedback to come automatically. No one wants to disappoint you with the bad news...until it's too late to do anything about it.

Real, honest feedback violates the "physics" of organizations. It is the flow of information uphill. As such, you must install "pumps," or processes beforehand to ensure that this vital information will flow to the top. Specific timeframes, formats, vehicles, and requirements for feedback must be established prior to taking action.

4. *Adjust and Adapt:* Be prepared to make alterations. No plan is perfect. Protect the integrity and the purpose of the change by "giving" quickly on small issues that make little difference.

The extent to which you are successful in the "monitoring" and "feedback" steps is the extent to which you will be able to select the correct place and means to adjust. The data you act upon will be mostly "soft" at this time. Hard data—test scores, dropout figures, absent rates—will not be available this early in the change process. And by the time you have this type of data, it will be too late to make the subtle shifts that can make or break a program.

This, then, is a critical juncture.

You must rely on "soft data" and intuition; at times to stand firm, and at other times be flexible.

This is why your hand must always be on the pulse of what's happening. Too often, in our experience, administrators and staffs spin dramatic change out there and assume that it will take. The odds are strongly against this happening.

The change you have initiated is a delicate seedling. It needs nurturing and constant attention. Too much or too little water or sun or nutrients and it will die.

Then, there are the naysayers. Those who will abandon ship at the first sign of a storm...or even a bad weather report. They will come to you in droves telling you how they knew it really wouldn't work from the start. Please, they are saying, let's go back to the old ways; it was so much more comfortable.

Make no mistake: this is a critical time! And this is when strong leadership shines. Remember—

If it were easy, somebody already would have done it!

5. *Communicate:* It is almost a statement of the obvious that it is essential to let everyone—all constituencies—know what is going on. No cute prose here. Let them know the good, the bad, and the ugly. Develop a means, some kind of a daily bulletin, to convey what is happening. In some instances, we have used a simple page with a line drawn vertically in the middle listing the "pluses" on one side and the "minuses" on the other.

But, regardless of the format you use, each day must conclude with an assessment of gains and problems. Design strategies to deal with the problems. Tomorrow you'll see if they work. Gradually, you will build a "chronicle of successes" that will attest to the growth that has occurred.

Taking action, then, is a concentrated, focused effort aggressively undertaken by people who believe they can make change happen. They are empowered. Not just because they have taken action, but, just as important, because they have set the stage, created the environment, and developed the plans prior to taking action.

These are the exciting times for movers and shakers! But this is not the moment for the faint hearted to be at the controls.

STEP 6 CHECKLIST

- ☐ Implement tactical plans
- ☐ Monitor
- ☐ Receive Feedback
- ☐ Adjust/Adapt
- ☐ Communicate current status (continually)

STEP 7

MOVE TO THE NEXT LEVEL

- *OBSERVATION: "Learning...A Little Bit Like Electricity"*

- *MOVE TO THE NEXT LEVEL*

- *STEP 7 CHECKLIST*

I have never let my schooling interfere with my education.

Mark Twain

OBSERVATION:

Learning...A Little Bit Like Electricity

Learning is often called a "lifelong activity." Learning is more than that. Learning is a life-sustaining activity. Learning enables us to continually grow and adapt to ever-changing circumstances. In a continual search to categorize and de-mystify education, we have attempted to define and delimit learning as a formal process, consciously undertaken, to acquire some predetermined skill or knowledge. Unwittingly, in our arrogant need to classify and understand, we have taken the wonder from learning.

Plato considered all learning "re-learning." Learning, according to Plato, was a process wherein man overcame the physical barriers of the body and rediscovered what the mind and soul already knew.[1] Aristotle viewed learning as a cooperative enterprise between the mind and body. The extent to which the Greeks, as well as other societies, valued learning was evidenced by the high esteem in which they held teachers. Learning was a sanctified, wondrous, and even mystical undertaking.

In the 20th century, we have demeaned the term education and relegated the process to a rather mundane, tedious, and daily task.

But learning is truly a wonder, a daily miracle. We really never see learning and can only conjecture what actually goes

---

[1] The term "educate" comes from Plato's concept of learning. Educate is derived from the combination of two latin words—duco, meaning to lead and "e" meaning to draw forth. Education, then, was the process of leading a person to draw forth from within what he or she already knew. Plato's dialogues are a self-discovery process in which the teacher, through a questioning technique, enables the student to draw from within that knowledge which already resides there.

on within the learner. A little bit like electricity. When I flip the light switch, I have taken the final step in a series of events emanating from spillways in the mountains, or generators hidden in the bowels of huge dams, or steam turbines at work. All I know is that when I flip that switch, my room is illuminated. All that engineers and scientists really know is that under the correct conditions, this unseen force—electricity—does, indeed, abide by certain laws of physics, and can be transmitted to ultimately illuminate my room.

In its own way, learning remains a similar mystery. But, whereas scientists and engineers have determined certain laws governing the generation and transmission of electricity, educators have never been able to establish what makes learning happen. We have, it appears, deceived ourselves into believing that certain actions cause learning to occur. I question whether we have "caused" learning or whether it would have happened anyway, sometimes in spite of our actions.

For example, take a look at how we have defined and categorized learning. See if this is consistent with natural learning. We train teachers to break down the whole into small bite-sized parts. In turn, they analyze or take apart the key components and hand them one at a time to the child.

Now, suppose we used this method in teaching our children how to walk.[1] First, we would spend three or four weeks asking the child to raise only the left leg. Once he or she had that skill down, we would then teach the child how to put the foot on the floor. Next we would spend weeks or months teaching how to raise the right leg in a timely manner. We would spend endless hours on the flex of the foot, the flex of the knee, and the correct posture. Finally, after teaching this and all other aspects of walking, we would ask a very confused child to take a full step or two.

---

[1] I am indebted to my mentor, Dudley Igo, for this example.

Taking this analogy to its extreme, parents would be taught the bell curve of learning. That is, they would be informed that a small portion of students would very quickly master walking, a majority would gradually master it, and others would not master it at all. Educators would then place time constraints on learning to walk. Each child would have 12 months, or 11 months (or whatever the median was) to learn how to walk (with the help of our expert instruction). If some did not master walking during that time, we would stop teaching, determine that they were at the wrong end of the bell curve, and order lifetime wheelchairs.

They failed walking.

And for the rest of their lives, they would function under this handicap, because obviously, any child who had not mastered walking in the prescribed timeframe, (with the help of our expert, step-by-step instruction) certainly would never be able to master walking.

Of course, walking is a wholly unified motion to be learned as such. Once a child's physical body—muscles, joints, bones, and nerves—are ready, he will choose behavior that makes the most sense in getting around. At best, our help and assistance do not hinder the process. On some occasions, it may even help. But when the conditions for learning are in place, the magic of learning occurs on its own. The entire act of walking one step after another, lifting the leg, putting the leg down, balancing, are learned as part of one orchestrated motion rather than as a series of isolated steps.

Take the art of writing as the classroom equivalent. For years we have taught, through the rules of grammar, a set of principles abstracted from the art as a whole. We teach children punctuation, capitalization, spelling, verb agreement, sentence diagraming, and when we put it all together, do we have writing?

The answer is an emphatic "NO!" What we have is conformity to certain rules and usages. What we have is the form, not the essence, of writing.

To understand the essence of writing, one must read, write, receive feedback, understand logical concepts, and with any luck at all, feel from the soul and seek ways to convey those feelings.

However we define writing, there is little argument as to what it is not; it is not the punctuation, spelling, or any of the other rules and conformities listed above.

People in the arts seem to understand this concept more than others, though even they, at times, reduce the wonder of the whole to the workaday summation of the parts. I recall reading that Andrew Lloyd-Weber, of *Phantom of the Opera* and other musical fame, was advised by his father to drop out of a very prestigious music school in London. His music was beginning to sound indistinguishable as it conformed to rules and accepted practices he was being taught.

Teaching, as we know it today, was strongly influenced by the scientific management movement in America. Its origins lay in the efforts of Henry Ford who broke car assembly into numerous component activities. The artist who had formerly taken pride in the creation of the entire automobile was replaced by assembly-line workers who routinely repeated the same task. The art and joy of learning have similarly been compromised by our tendency to break down complex, inter-related actions into assembly-line types of activities.

Please do not misunderstand me. It is certainly necessary to master multiplication as well as division before one takes on quadratic equations. But while there is need for practice, the teacher who assigns students 65 more problems only to ensure they know how to multiply, probably ensures that the students will hate multiplication—or at least find it dull and boring.

How often do we demand that the child who has learned the magic of tying her shoe repeat this task 65 times? Children enjoy mastering a skill and practice it until such time as the need for practice no longer exists; and so it should be with all learning.

But, our most grave error in teaching building-block skills is that of failing to mention the whole, failing to describe the ultimate purpose of the activity. How often do we teach punctuation, capitalization, or sentence structure by first bringing children into contact with great literature and then explaining to them that mastering the mechanics will enable them to communicate like this? Why not start every second grade punctuation lesson with an example from great literature so that the child can understand and appreciate the value of tools being taught.

We have great distance to retrace and much damage to undo if we are to recapture the magic and excitement of learning. Fortunately, because this magic is integral to growth and life itself, children do continue to enjoy new and exciting experiences. Unfortunately, with the exception of a few classrooms in each school, this excitement is limited to non-formal educational experiences. It's not simply that teachers don't understand or lack the will. It's because our schools, as well as our classrooms, were developed on a factory-like model. Despite all the scientific and technological advances going on around us, schools have strayed little from this mass-production model. That's why we group children in lots of thirty; that's why we break down knowledge and learning into component parts; that's why we divide these parts throughout the curriculum in much the same way as the assembly-line divides tasks; and that's why time is such an important condition placed on learning.

To rediscover the magic of learning, we need a new mindset and a different paradigm. It is extremely difficult for the individual teacher or principal while working within the constraints of the factory-model school to turn up the voltage and to admit humbly to the electric mystery of learning.

Yet, this is precisely what needs to happen. We must begin to rediscover the mystery of learning. To do this means breaking down the barriers of the old learning approaches. Traditions die hard, these are well past senility.

It's time to bring back the magic.

STEP 7: MOVE TO THE NEXT LEVEL

Successful schools exhibit a spiral of ongoing change on all fronts—instruction, behavior, curriculum—rather than on one thing one year and another the next. Upon arrival at a predetermined benchmark (and this may occur at six months or a year), the school needs to assess its progress, revisit its strategic plan, and begin to formulate its next level of action on each front. Schools that attempt to complete all change in one year will be sadly disappointed. Dynamic schools, by their very nature, continually assess, learn, and improve.

Evaluative tasks should be assigned to individuals and groups responsible for change in a certain area. They should not only assess progress but update the tactical plan. Potential problems are again identified and failsafe methodology utilized to identify "root causes." The final product is an updated, revised strategic action plan, achieved through various tactics that dictate specific actions. Sound confusing? This is simply a return to Step 5—Generate A Blueprint for Action.

But the process of revisiting the strategic plan is more than a formality. It forces the school to re-establish its priorities and rededicate its energies. It provides a time to reflect on progress made, changes in process, and problems that have been overcome. It is a chance to assimilate all that has been learned and apply it to the next level. In many instances, schools have used this as an opportunity to thank and reward staff, to pat each other on the back.

Orchestrated correctly, Move to the Next Level serves as both an end and a beginning. At the completion of the first year, looking back can be an especially energizing and inspirational experience.

STEP 7 CHECKLIST

- ❏ Assess progress at prescribed benchmark
- ❏ Communicate progress
- ❏ Revisit strategic plan
- ❏ Return to Steps 5 & 6

IV

THAT'S IT!

There you have it: the 7 Steps to School Change and the preconditions that set the stage. Apply them as a unified process and you will see and feel the growth. Each is necessary. Don't short-circuit the system by avoiding those steps which are particularly difficult to address in your current situation.

I confess, that after reading this, it sounds more complicated than it is. It's simple, basic stuff. After you get into it, you'll feel the logic and rationale for each step. We learned the critical need for each step the hard way. Don't make the same mistake.

If you're sincere about making change, but are experiencing difficulty relating the 7 Step Process to your school, relax.

The checklist on the next pages may help. Otherwise, review the steps individually...and, if all else fails or if none of it seems to make sense, give me a call, maybe I can help.

As far as I'm concerned, what you're embarking upon—school change—is the most important undertaking not only of your life, but of the lives of thousands of students who will experience the revitalized instruction, meaningful curriculum, and purpose-charged environment which you have created for them.

You will impact the course of their lives, provide hope where there is despair; light where there is darkness, and a future where none now exists...all because you had the courage to act boldly against what at times seemed insurmountable odds.

Congratulations...you are indeed the Modern American Hero.

THE 7 STEPS CHECKLIST

PRECONDITIONS
A. *Local Autonomy*
❏ Assess the school's parameters of authority
B. *Leadership Growth Potential*
❏ Create leadership growth profile of chief administrator(s)
C. *Staff Readiness*
❏ Assess the level of staff dissatisfaction
❏ Assess staff goal alignment

STEP 1. CREATE A "CHANGE" MINDSET
❏ Generate the belief that change is possible
❏ Create a vision

STEP 2. DETERMINE THE METHOD OF SCOREKEEPING
❏ Construct a meaningful assessment model
❏ Determine the instruments to be used
❏ Streamline the collection and reporting of data

STEP 3. ESTABLISH A LEVEL PLAYING FIELD
❏ Develop the rationale for discipline
❏ Determine the underlying principles
❏ Establish the social contract
❏ Understand the 80/20 time trap

☐ Streamline policies and procedures
☐ Ensure consistent application of rules

STEP 4.   DEVELOP ORGANIZATIONAL READINESS
☐ Adjust administrative/organizational structure
☐ Construct an effective decision analysis framework
☐ Facilitate data collection/handling/access

STEP 5.   GENERATE A BLUEPRINT FOR ACTION
☐ Review the Mission
☐ Assess current "results"
☐ Clearly spell out the new intended results
☐ Create a plan to achieve the results
☐ Face reality: *Most Plans Fail*
☐ Identify the resisting forces within the environment
☐ Failsafe the plan

STEP 6.   TAKE ACTION
☐ Implement tactical plans
☐ Monitor
☐ Receive Feedback
☐ Adjust/Adapt
☐ Communicate current status (continually)

STEP 7.   MOVE TO THE NEXT LEVEL
☐ Assess progress at prescribed benchmark
☐ Communicate progress
☐ Revisit strategic plan
☐ Return to Steps 5 & 6

V

AN OPEN LETTER TO
CORPORATE AMERICA

Dear Mr./Ms. CEO:

I challenge you. No, I dare you.

Take a detour off the beaten path of your corporate world into mine, the world of your customers, your clients, your employees of the year 2000.

Come with me to the eastsides, southsides, the projects and the migrant camps. Drive through the littered, violent streets. Look at the youth leaning back, knee flexed, shoe pressed flat against the wall. See the hopeless future smoldering in his eyes.

This is my world, the youth of today, the adults of tomorrow. And these are your clients, your customers, your employees of the year 2000. They are the "market" and the "human resources" in your strategic plan.

Look at the numbers. The cost of providing each of these youth with a luxury automobile pales in comparison to the dollars you will spend on them in welfare, unemployment, public housing, drug rehabilitation, criminal justice, incarceration, and a myriad of other social programs, some yet to be invented. Three-quarters of all prison inmates are school dropouts.

These kids live for today with one single thought: survival. In reality, there is no place for them in your long-range strategic plan.

Strictly from an economic point of view, however, these numbers are too large to dismiss. From the human and moral perspective, these numbers are unconscionable.

For these young people there is only one way out: EDUCATION. Education represents the greatest return on investment for corporate America between now and the turn of the century. For many, schools are the only means of escape from the cycle of poverty and dependence. Education remains the cornerstone of the American Dream.

But, you ask, are we not describing here the worst examples? Aren't youth in the suburbs and rural America o.k.? Aren't schools there working well?

Are they?

Youth in suburbia need serious help if they are to compete in the global economy of the year 2000.

In science, for example, the U.S. ranked fifth out of the six nations tested—ahead of Ireland, but behind Spain, Canada, the U.K. and Korea. In math, the U.S. was dead last among the same nations. In 1989, the leading U.S. patent winners were, in order, Hitachi, Toshiba, Canon, G.E., Fuji, Phillips, and Siemans.

But, you may further ask, hasn't corporate America been pouring money into Education...at least since the publication of "A Nation at Risk" in 1983?

The answer is yes, (although "pouring" might be an over-statement). Nonetheless, significant sums have been contributed to public education.

Most of this money, in reality, has had little impact on what happens in the classroom and ultimately to children. To impact public education, corporate America must do more than give money, it must commit its resources and its influence to redesigning America's education delivery system—the school. Blue ribbon committees and governors' conferences may spur a new level of public consciousness, but the trickle-down effect on schools is almost nil.

——————

During the past thirteen years, we have been fortunate to work with schools in a variety of settings across the country. We approach our work with ten basic beliefs about the state of American Education and what it takes to bring about substantive change. Corporate America, I believe, should take heed.

1. Schools are everyone's problem.

The statistics from our schools are frightening. While it is recognized that our nation's schools are in trouble, it is much less understood that our work force, our economy, and the very fabric of our society are threatened as a result.

2. Money alone is not the answer.

Schools have been an issue since the publication of "A Nation at Risk" in 1983. This report spawned a variety of Blue Ribbon Committees and task forces resulting in a proliferation of confirming reports and calls to action. In addition, these reports paved the way for the influx of corporate and foundation dollars into schools. But in terms of outcomes, there have been no significant changes. In fact, the only observable growth in schools in the past ten years has been in the area of "increased violence."

3. "More of the same" is not the answer: Schools must substantively change how they do business if they're to become successful.

There are two ways to bring about improvement: quantitative change and qualitative change. Quantitative change is based on the premise that what we need is more of the same. It assumes that the system is inherently sound, but simply lacks the capital or the resources to perform effectively.

Qualitative change recognizes that the system itself is the problem. Its separate parts work in confusion rather than in concert, and its mission is continually compromised through the actions of individual units. Such is the case with our schools. In short, it is not a matter of dressing the wounds but of treating the infection.

4. Real change must begin at the school site.

Qualitative change cannot be imposed from above. A change in the "ethos" of the school, a realignment of its purpose, must spring from within the organization. It must start at the grass-roots level—the place where the product (learning) is delivered to the consumer (student).

5. If school change were easy, it would already have happened.

Society generally seeks simple answers to complex problems. School failure, then, is attributed to the "uncaring teachers," or "inept administrators," "single-parent homes," "working mothers," the "drug culture," "gang violence," etc.

Real causal factors, however, are typically "interactive." There is no single cause; rather it is the complex interplay between school and community, public agency and home, teacher and child, which makes for failure in our schools. Just as there are no simplistic causes, there are no quick and easy solutions.

6. Schools need a change process.

Most parents do care about their children; most teachers can teach; most administrators can run effective schools. What they don't know how to do is change schools. They have no background or training in how to make ineffective schools into effective schools. There is no roadmap to guide them through the complexities of organizational change, no systematic process to identify and address the truly critical issues.

7. The change process must enable the school to start from "ground zero" and rebuild itself into an effective and efficient operation.

Schools must redefine their mission, reallocate their resources, and rededicate their energies to create an environment in which teachers can teach and students can learn. There is only one way this can occur: start from the beginning; define the purpose, create a system that works.

8. The change process must be characterized by openness and integrity, and generate the focus and consensus necessary for action.

The change process must not only address the interactive influences of the various constituencies, it must also join staff and community into a common enterprise utilizing grass-roots input in developing the "roadmap" for change. Together, staff and community, must separate the important from the trivial and the general from the special interest. They must target the school's resources and focus its energies on the things that will make a difference.

9. Change is disruptive.

Change is never easy. Real and meaningful change goes to the very heart of a system, threatens the comfort of the status quo, and elicits the full range of human emotions.

Qualitative change, by its very nature, exposes the core of the organization. In so doing, the system's weaknesses, its shortcomings, its inconsistencies, its contradictions, its inadequacies, and its various levels of competence are revealed. It should be anticipated, then, that a process directed at bringing about such change will be traumatic.

But this trauma also marks a new beginning; a new sense of purpose; a new spirit of belief that things can be different—that the system can work.

10. Schools can change

Based on our experience in developing and field testing the *7 Steps to School Change* in over 175 schools in various environments across the country, I know that schools can change.

But schools do not exist in isolation; and the reason more schools do not change is because they lack the community structure to both support and demand change. If schools across the country are to change, corporate America, as part of the local and "national" community, must become a major player.

————

I suggest, then, Mr. or Ms. CEO, that you consider amending your strategic plan to include a commitment, financial and otherwise, to the education of your future clients and future employees—the students of the 90's so that they will have the knowledge and skills to create, produce, as well as consume your products and services of the year 2000....I suggest that you get serious about restructuring America's schools and begin to treat education as the crisis that it is—that you begin to bring to it your energy, your resources, your expertise, your commitment, your support...because the cost of preserving America's future is nothing compared to the cost of not having one.

Sincerely,
Joe Petterle
Sacramento, California
1993

Look for all these and other fine Kantar Books
at your favorite bookstore or write to:

KANTAR ON BRIDGE

Edwin B. Kantar is a world-renowned author on bridge, and winner of many national and international tournaments.

The books available here are not meant for beginners, nor are they aimed at experts. They are directed at players somewhere between these extremes who would like to improve their game substantially. Could this be you?

	PRICE	QTY.	AMOUNT
Take Your Tricks	$11.95		
A Treasury of Bridge Tips – Bidding	$10.95		
A New Approach to Play and Defense (Vol. 1)	$10.95		
A New Approach to Play and Defense (Vol. 2)	$10.95		
	Sub-total		
	CA res. add 8.25%		
	Shipping		
	TOTAL		

Shipping: 1st book, $2.00
Add'l books, $1.00 each

Please enclose check or
money order made payable to:
Eddie Kantar

Send order to:
Eddie Kantar
P.O. Box 427
Venice, CA 90291-0427

Look for these financial and other fine Griffin Books
at your favorite bookstore or write to:

GRIFFIN PUBLISHING

(Please Print)   Date _____

Name _____

Address _____

City _____ State _____ Zip _____

Phone (_____) _____

	PRICE	QTY.	AMOUNT
Starting to Plan for Lifetime Financial Independence Elmo A. Petterle A workbook designed to provide you with financial, retirement and estate planning.	$17.95		
Workers' Compensation Abuse Robert J. Frasco and John Simmers An employer's guide to combating fraud through early intervention investigation.	$49.95		
Future Force – Kids That Want To, Can, and Do! Carolyn Wicks and Elaine McClanahan This book offers a program for improving skills of children to parents, teachers, and students.	$19.95		
You're Not Over Drawn — Just Underdeposited Beverlee Kelley A simple solution to organizing and maintaining control over your finances.	$12.95		
Entreprenuerial Transitions: From Inspired Genuis to Visionary Leader Roy F. Cammarano Manage your organization for what you want it to become . . . not for what it is and ***never*** for what it was.	$16.95		
	Sub-total		
	CA res. add 8.25%		
	Shipping		
	TOTAL		

Shipping: 1st book, $2.00
Add'l books, $1.00 each

Check type of payment:
____ Check or
        money order enclosed
____ Visa   ____ Mastercard

Acct. # _____

Exp. Date _____

Signature _____

Send order to:
**Griffin Publishing
544 W. Colorado St.
Glendale, CA 91204**
Or call to order:
**1-800-423-5789 CA
1-800-826-4849 USA**